AMAZING
MYSTERIES
OF THE WORLD

BY CATHERINE O'NEILL

BOOKS FOR WORLD EXPLORERS
NATIONAL GEOGRAPHIC SOCIETY

CONTENTS

Copyright © 1983 National Geographic Society
Library of Congress ⊂ℙ Data: page 104

Cover: Dancing bands of light glow in the sky above Fairbanks, Alaska. Scientists know the sun's energy creates the northern lights. Indians once said the lights came from the fires of the "Great Spirit."
LEE SNYDER/GEOPHYSICAL INSTITUTE/UNIVERSITY OF ALASKA, FAIRBANKS

Title page: Comet West streams through the sky in 1976. Its orbit around the sun is so great that it might not return to the vicinity of earth for a million years.
DENNIS DI CICCO/SKY & TELESCOPE

Did you ever hear someone say, "It's raining cats and dogs"? If so, that person was simply describing a hard rain. But if you ever hear someone say that it's raining fish, you'd better go out and look. Though it doesn't happen often, fish have actually fallen with rain in different places all over the world. This painting (right) shows what a fall of fish in the northwestern part of the United States might look like. How is it possible that fish fall from the sky? Strong whirlwinds, called tornadoes or waterspouts, pick up fish from water like a vacuum cleaner picking up dust. The winds can carry the fish a long way before dropping them.
SALLY J. BENSUSEN

CHAPTER 1

WHAT IS A MYSTERY?

For centuries, people have been wondering about the world around them and trying to explain the amazing things that happen on the earth and in the sky. Take eclipses, for instance. How do you think you would explain an eclipse of the sun if you had no way of knowing what actually happens during an eclipse? The ancient Chinese believed that as the sun disappeared a dragon was eating it. They beat drums to scare the dragon away—and, sure enough, the sun reappeared.

Today, people know that such a belief is not true. Now there is a scientific explanation for what happens. The sun disappears because once in a while—as the moon and the earth move in their orbits—the moon comes between the earth and the sun. It's as if you moved your hand (the moon) between your head (the earth) and an electric light (the sun). This book explains how scientists continually search for answers to the world's mysteries.

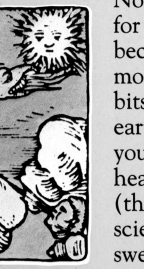

A dragon gobbles the sun in an old print. The Chinese of long ago believed this was what happened during eclipses of the sun.
PETER BELLEW

Only a thin edge of the sun remains visible at the height of a partial eclipse (right). In a total solar eclipse, the moon would hide the sun.
HORST SCHAFER/PHOTO TRENDS

SEARCHING FOR ANSWERS

CARLO MAURI

The Tigris (above) proved that ancient people could have sailed great distances. Norwegian explorer Thor Heyerdahl built the boat. He used reeds that grow where the Tigris and Euphrates Rivers join in southwest Asia. His boat is like those he saw in 4,000-year-old pictures. Heyerdahl found he could sail 4,200 miles (6,759 km)* from Iraq to the east coast of Africa. Sailors long ago might also have done it.

How do scientists and other people with new ideas prove that their ideas are true?

Personal observation is one way. For instance, many people once thought that the world was flat and that it ended at the horizon. Not until explorers sailed around the earth did people actually observe that a ship never reaches the horizon and learn that the earth is shaped like a huge ball.

Doing or seeing something, and keeping records to describe it—that's how scientists operate. Astronomer Fred L. Whipple, for example, is eagerly awaiting the reappearance of Halley's comet in 1986. Halley's comet reappears every 76 years or so. Dr. Whipple, who has studied comets for years, believes that comets are "dirty snowballs" from space, composed of ice, dust, and gases. Most astronomers agree with him.

Spacecraft will approach Halley's comet during its next appearance and make measurements with special instruments. Then Dr. Whipple will have one more excellent chance to see if he's right or wrong. Dr. Whipple will report his findings to the world. Everyone will then know more about comets.

Sometimes scientists don't live to see their

*Metric figures in this book have been rounded off.

For many centuries, people believed that the sun and everything in the heavens revolved about the earth. But the astronomer Nicolaus Copernicus (left) had another idea. He carefully studied the movements of the stars and planets. He came to believe that the earth and the other planets revolve about the sun. Most of the people who lived during his time thought Copernicus was wrong. But later, the invention of the telescope helped prove that his model of the solar system, shown in the chart on his desk, is correct. We know a lot more about the solar system than Copernicus did, but he had the basic idea almost 500 years ago.

A hundred years ago, horse owners often discussed the question: Do all four feet of a fast-moving horse leave the ground at the same time? Pictures (below) by the English-born photographer Eadweard Muybridge proved that they do. Muybridge set up a row of cameras that took pictures a split second apart. Before seeing this photographic proof, people could only guess how a running horse's feet move. The feet move too fast for human eyes to follow.

ideas proved or disproved. Years later, other scientists may discover new ways to test old observations. That's what happened to Nicolaus Copernicus. In 1543, the Polish astronomer published his theory that the sun, not the earth, was the center of the solar system. Galileo Galilei, an Italian astronomer, proved the theory in 1609 by using the newly invented telescope to get a closer look.

At other times, people try to prove that an idea *could* be true. Explorer Thor Heyerdahl did that when he built the *Tigris*, a boat of reeds. He did not prove that ancient people actually sailed across the Arabian Sea from Asia to Africa; he proved they *could* have.

People who seek to explain mysteries must be willing to explore all the possibilities and to take chances. They must accept the risk of being wrong without becoming discouraged.

When scientists want to learn how something happens, they observe the event, gathering as much information about it as possible. The tools scientists use may be as simple as pencils and notebooks for writing down their

Is this animal (above) part giraffe and part zebra? No. It's an okapi (oh-KOP-ee), a mammal scientists didn't even know existed until about 1900. It was then that European explorers obtained okapi skins from tribespeople who lived in central Africa's rain forests.

observations, or as complex as powerful telescopes for looking beyond the Milky Way. Scientists use compasses, computers, cameras, and many other kinds of equipment. Two of the best tools a mystery-solver uses are invisible: imagination and patience.

"True" things sometimes turn out to be false, as scientists use new methods to study old theories. Sometimes, things that many people believe to be imaginary turn out to be real. For example, many years ago well-educated Europeans thought that reports

Is it a duck or a beaver? Neither. It's a platypus (PLAT-ih-pus), a strange, egg-laying mammal (below) that lives in Australia. When explorers brought a platypus skin to England in 1798, people could hardly believe their eyes. A furry animal with a ducklike bill, webbed feet, and a tail like a beaver's? Impossible! But later, when scientists actually saw live platypuses, they knew the explorers' tales had to be true.

In Europe, until late in the 18th century, most people had never seen giraffes (left). Even though Greek and Roman writings contained descriptions of the spotted, long-necked animals, many people thought they were imaginary. Today, people know that giraffes are real—every inch of them!

9

about large stones falling from the sky were just tall tales of superstitious peasants.

Then one day in 1803, about two thousand stones fell on a town in France. Observers had to admit that the stories seemed true. They realized that these stones and others like them might have come from space. Today, we know that stones from space do strike the earth. We call such stones meteorites. Recently, scientists studied a meteorite that fell long ago in Antarctica. They learned that it probably came from the moon.

Mysteries don't have to come from space, however. They exist right here on earth. About 200 years ago, when people in Africa told stories about hairy animals that looked somewhat like people, biologists didn't believe them. Finally, a French-born explorer brought back the body of a gorilla, proving that the stories were true. Today, gorillas do not seem unusual. Many zoos have them.

Maybe the discovery of the gorilla helps to explain why people haven't given up looking for Bigfoot, or Sasquatch, a large, ape-like creature that some observers say they have seen in the forests of the northwestern United States and western Canada. Scientists have photographs to study and footprints in the mud and snow to puzzle over. But they still want to see hard evidence—a live animal or at least some bones.

Many mysteries remain to be solved in your own backyard, in the ocean, and in space. Searching for answers sometimes reveals surprising things—as you'll see while exploring the rest of this book.

This is not just a mouselike animal. It's a living fossil (above). Only tiny 20,000-year-old bones proved that mountain pygmy possums ever existed—until searchers found a live one in Australia in 1966.

A coelacanth (SEE-luh-canth) looks like a prehistoric monster in the depths of the ocean (right). Until 1938, scientists thought this large fish was extinct. Then fishermen in the Indian Ocean caught a live one.

10

11

CHAPTER 2

THE WORLD AROUND US

For many centuries, people have looked up to see mysterious, shimmering "northern lights" in the night sky. Eskimos in Alaska once believed that the lights were the spirits of seals, caribou, and whales. Algonquian Indians of Canada and the northeastern United States thought that the lights were reflections from a huge fire built by the "Great Spirit."

Long ago, the northern lights sometimes frightened people who believed they were a sign of bad times to come. In 1583, for instance, when the eerie lights glowed high in the skies over France, people flocked to churches to pray.

The northern lights still look awesome. But today scientists know that they are natural, not supernatural. The following pages give explanations of the northern lights, of other strange lights, and of previously unknown life far beneath the sea where light never reaches.

Northern lights paint the Canadian sky with dazzling color. The event can also affect the flow of electricity in power lines.
COURTESY OF A.T.Y. LUI

Feathery fingers of light reach toward a house in Fairbanks, Alaska (right). Turn the page to learn what causes such awesome displays.
CLIFF HOLLENBECK

13

One night in A.D. 37, over the Italian colony of Ostia, the northern lights suddenly appeared. People outside Ostia thought the buildings and homes were on fire, so they hurried to help. This fiery picture of Fairbanks, Alaska (left), shows why the people might have been frightened.

Usually, only people who live in or near the Arctic, or scientists in Antarctica, see strange lights glowing in the sky high above the highest clouds. But sometimes the auroras (uh-ROAR-uz), as they are called, spread far outward from the Poles. During the early 1980s in the United States, people living as far south as the Mexican border reported seeing the lights.

Scientists think that periods of intense activity on the surface of the sun may cause the streaming lights to appear at such low latitudes. Why the sun? Because that's where the action begins that turns on the polar sky show.

The sun is never still. Superhot gas constantly flows up from the surface, streaming far out into space. High temperatures cause the atoms that form the gas to change and to become electrically charged particles.

The charged particles speed from the sun in all directions, traveling hundreds of miles per second. The particles form what is called the solar wind. It takes about four days for solar wind to reach the outer edges of the earth's

Fiery skies. In 1958, a strong display of northern lights stained skies red from the Arctic as far south as Cuba. This time exposure shows the slanted tracks left by stars above the Geophysical Institute of the University of Alaska at Fairbanks.

VIC HESSLER/UNIVERSITY OF ALASKA

15

magnetic field. The magnetic field extends far beyond the planet. Scientists think that the field is created by the movement of molten metal deep inside the earth. Like a bar magnet in which the magnetic force is concentrated at both ends of the magnet, earth's magnetism is strongest at its magnetic poles.

The north magnetic pole and the south magnetic pole are not the same as the North Pole and the South Pole. The north magnetic pole lies in northern Canada, about a thousand miles (1,609 km) south of the geographic North Pole. Compasses point to the spot.

The magnetic field is invisible. If you could see it, you would see lines of magnetic energy extending in huge loops from the north magnetic pole to the south magnetic pole all

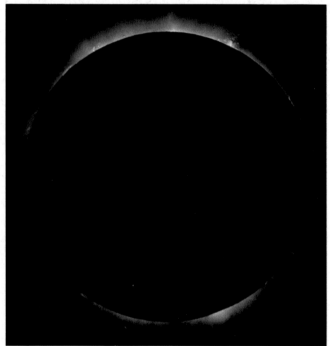

JAY M. PASACHOFF AND MARTIN S. WEINHAUS

Sometimes the gases that form the sun erupt with tremendous force, sending solar flares far into space (left). Such flares increase the solar wind so that it disturbs the earth's magnetic field and helps create lights in the sky. Added color brings out more of the detail in this picture taken by a solar telescope on Skylab. During a total solar eclipse (above), the moon blocks out the sun but leaves the flares exposed.

NASA/SKYLAB

17

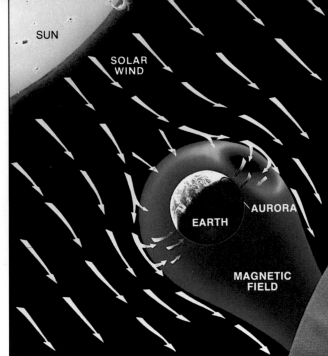

around the planet, shielding the earth in a sort of magnetic envelope. This envelope protects the earth from the charged particles that continuously flow from the sun.

As the solar wind moves toward earth, most of its particles are turned aside by the magnetic field to sweep past the planet. Some particles, however, do enter the field and are trapped. These particles spiral around the lines of magnetic energy and bounce between the magnetic poles. As they do, some of them collide with atoms of air in the earth's upper atmosphere. Collisions between charged solar particles and atoms of oxygen and nitrogen in the atmosphere produce the green, red, violet, and blue lights called auroras.

It takes a lot of energy to "turn on" the auroras. Sometimes one display makes use of as much power as the people of the United States use in one day. Such large amounts of power can interfere with communications systems on earth. The charged particles bouncing around in the earth's magnetic field can confuse radio signals: Alaskan taxi drivers have received radio calls dispatched in New Jersey!

The atmospheric disturbance caused by the particles can make compasses point the wrong way, cause power failures, and interfere with computers aboard satellites.

Scientists seek answers to many questions about the auroras. International teams of scientists have launched satellites specially designed to study the still mysterious lights, and more experiments are planned.

The earth's magnetic field shields us from charged solar particles called the solar wind (above). As the particles flow toward the earth, most are turned aside by the magnetic field and sweep around the planet. But some do enter the field and leak into the earth's upper atmosphere. Most of these particles enter the atmosphere near the magnetic poles. Collisions between solar particles and atoms of air in the earth's upper atmosphere produce the colorful lights called auroras (uh-ROAR-uz).

Photographed from a satellite 10,000 miles (16,093 km) away, the northern lights look like a red halo resting on the earth (right). Colors have been added to this picture, made in November 1981. This was a time when the northern lights were very bright. The aurora forms an oval extending over the Arctic region and beyond. In North America, the width of the band reaches from Chicago, Illinois, to Hudson Bay, in Canada, a distance of 1,300 miles (2,092 km). An artist outlined the land areas. Sunlight on the other side of the world shows up as blue over Asia and Europe at the top of the picture.

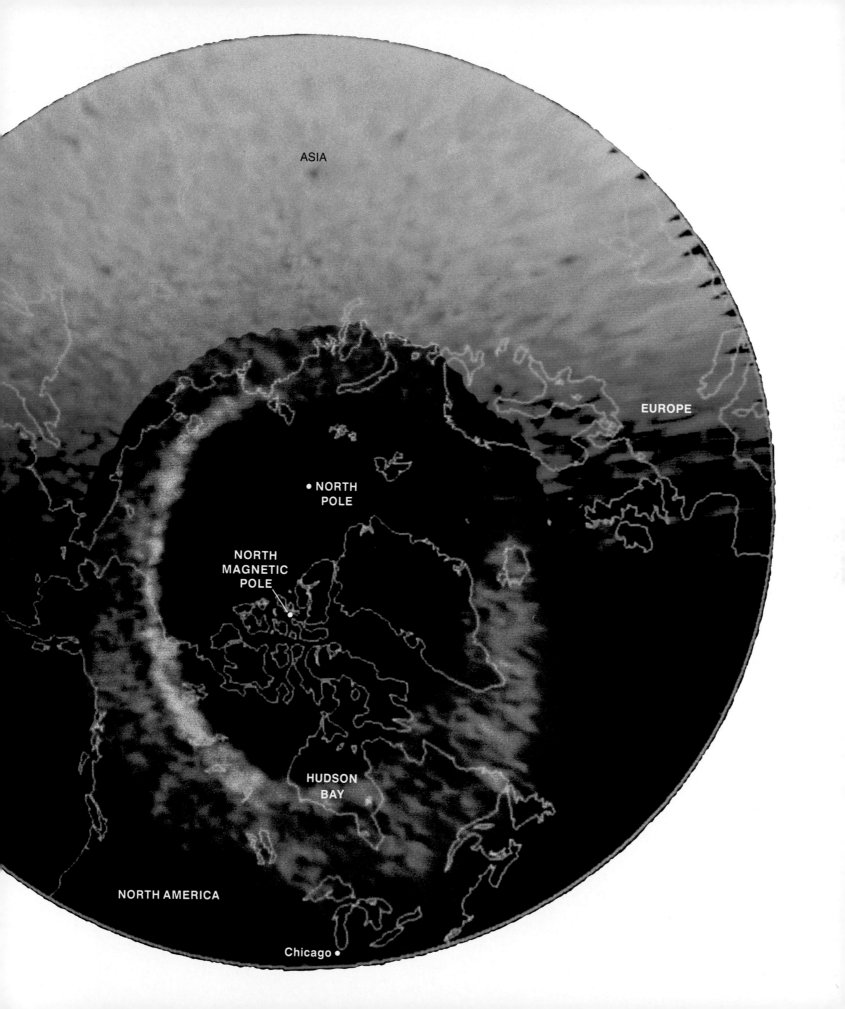

Ghostly lights that shine in swampy areas can be scary. But gases, not ghosts, cause swamp lights. Rotting plants give off the gases, which burn with a heat too low to start a forest fire. The lights may be flickering yellow, glowing blue, or fiery red.
ROBERT E. HYNES

GLOW FROM THE EARTH

We now know about light coming from the sky. But light from the ground?

People who live in swampy areas sometimes see strange lights glowing on or near the ground at night. At times the lights rise and float through the air. They may look like shiny balls of fire or tiny flames hugging the ground. In the past, people gave the lights names like "will-o'-the-wisp" or "jack-o'-lantern." They told ghost stories about them.

Scientists can now explain what causes the lights. In swamps and marshy areas, rotting plant life produces gases that can ignite. Sometimes lightning causes them to start burning. At other times the gases burn without even a spark to start them. They do not cause forest fires, however. Swamp gas fires glow, but produce only a little heat.

Earthquakes sometimes cause lights to glow near the ground. Here's what happens: During a large quake, pieces of the earth's crust grind together, creating an electric charge that gives off an eerie glow. Such lights have been seen from as far away as 70 miles (113 km).

Strange lights do not all come from the sky. The unusual pictures on this page show the glow that earthquakes sometimes cause. The pictures were taken in Japan. Some scientists say that heat created by rocks grinding together releases steam from the earth. The heat also generates an electric current. Together, steam and current make a bright glow for a minute or two after the most violent moments of the quake.

21

UNCHAINED POWER

Crash! Lightning shatters the sky during a summer thunderstorm. Anyone who has ever watched a thunderstorm has guessed that a lot of power is locked up in those flashing bolts of lightning, waiting to be unchained.

It's true. One average lightning bolt contains enough electricity to power a room air conditioner for two weeks.

Even before Benjamin Franklin attached a key to his kite, sent it up into a thunderstorm, and got a strong electric shock, people were fascinated by lightning. Today, nearly everyone knows that lightning is a form of electricity that builds up in thunderstorms, in dust storms, and in snowstorms.

Scientists still aren't sure how the electricity builds up. They don't know how to predict the path lightning will follow or how to predict exactly when it will strike.

Scientists who study the weather have spent years investigating lightning. In 1982, scientists at the State University of New York at Albany set up a system along the East Coast of the United States to keep track of how

Forks of lightning shoot from thunderclouds and strike the ground at the Grand Canyon, in Arizona. Every year, electricity that builds up in the atmosphere causes many millions of flashes like these. Scientists continue to search for the causes of this natural wonder.

22

many lightning bolts hit the ground each year, where they strike, and how much power each bolt contains.

During the summer of 1982, the system recorded 15,000 lightning bolts in a single storm—and those were only the ones that actually hit the ground. Lightning flashes in our atmosphere about two billion times every year. Around 40 bolts hit the Empire State Building in New York City each year, but lightning rods conduct the electricity safely into the ground.

We know that all lightning is basically the same. But it can take many shapes. Bolts may be forked, zigzagging for miles across the sky.

A flash of sheet lightning lights up a whole cloud for a second. Bead lightning, which looks like fireballs strung together, also lasts for a very short time. Ball lightning has been described as a fireball that apparently falls from a cloud and explodes as it hits the earth.

Scientists have developed techniques for producing lightning in the laboratory and are now working on creating ball lightning.

Rainbow of color spreads through the sky on either side of a lightning strike in Colorado (below). Special equipment sorts the lightning into bands of color, called a spectrum. The equipment also gives information about the gases formed within the lightning bolt.

Indoor lightning flashes in scientist Robert K. Golka's lab, in Wendover, Utah (above). To make the lightning, Golka connects a generator with a special coil 51 feet (16 m) in diameter. This produces lightning about one-fourth as strong as a natural bolt.

Like a necklace of beads, balls of lightning glow briefly above a model aircraft in Robert K. Golka's lab (left). This form of lightning—which lasts only a fraction of a second—is called bead lightning. Photographs indicate that the beadlike structure may form when an ordinary lightning path, or channel, collapses. Golka thinks the same process that causes bead lightning may lead to the formation of ball lightning.

25

WORLD WITHOUT SUN

The world's oceans hide an amazing landscape. Far below the waves lie huge mountain ranges and active volcanoes. In some places, molten rock from deep inside the earth flows up through cracks in the earth's crust. These cracks are called rifts.

Until recently, scientists could only guess at what the bottom of the sea was like. They believed that it was a cold, dark area that held little or no life. Sunlight can't reach to the depths of the ocean, miles below the surface. No sunlight plus extreme cold meant very little life—or so people thought.

Then in 1977, geologists riding in *Alvin*, a tiny submarine designed for deep dives, made a remarkable discovery. The scientists descended 8,500 feet (2,591 m) to reach the Galapagos Rift, a crack in the seafloor of the eastern Pacific Ocean. There *Alvin*'s bright headlights revealed an oasis crowded with life. Warm water gushed from vents in the ocean floor. And something in the warm water provided food to keep a huge variety of strange animals alive.

There were swaying, blood-red worms, some of them 12 feet (4 m) long. There were hundreds of mussels, and smooth-shelled clams as long as rulers. Lobsterlike crabs scuttled across the seafloor. Dandelion-shaped creatures anchored by delicate threads swayed

Jets of mineral-rich water shoot from the ocean floor. These jets are 650°F (343° C). This is so hot that when scientists first took temperature readings the thermometer's plastic mount melted.

Tiny bacteria thrive near warm-water vents. This photograph enlarges these life forms 1,100 times. Bacteria provide the basis of a food chain supplying larger and larger deep-sea animals.

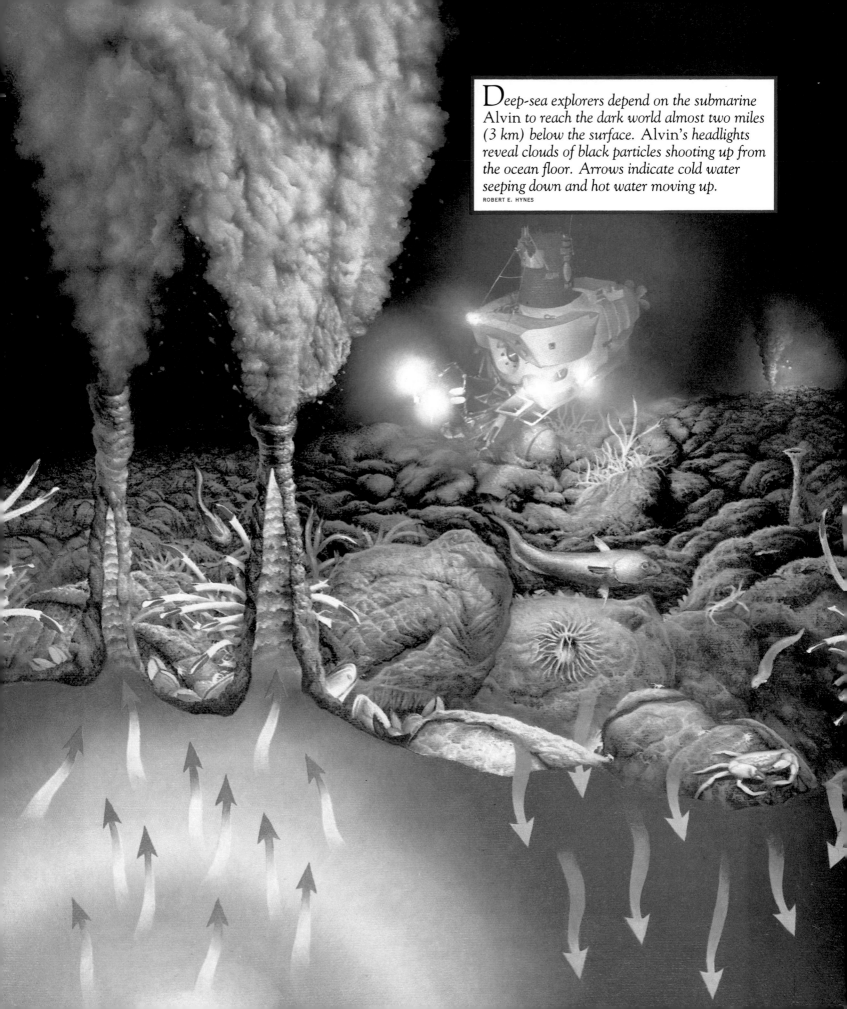

Deep-sea explorers depend on the submarine Alvin to reach the dark world almost two miles (3 km) below the surface. Alvin's headlights reveal clouds of black particles shooting up from the ocean floor. Arrows indicate cold water seeping down and hot water moving up.

ROBERT E. HYNES

in the water. Long, pinkish white fish hovered head down over warm springs that gushed from the bottom.

In 1979, at a similar location, the scientists found black clouds of superhot water pouring from chimney-shaped rock formations that looked like they might be the smokestacks of underwater factories.

Most of earth's living creatures depend on a process called photosynthesis (foto-SIN-thuh-sus). Plants make their own food with the aid of light, and animals eat the plants. But deep in the ocean, where the total darkness is never broken by the rays of the sun, tiny creatures called bacteria stay alive through the process of chemosynthesis (kee-mo-SIN-thuh-sus)— making food with the aid of chemical energy.

Until explorers spotted that first oasis on the ocean bottom, no one knew that so much life could exist without sunlight. Today, scientists who study the varied samples brought to the surface from the depths of the ocean are just beginning to understand how chemosynthesis works.

At the oasis, warm water spurts from within the earth. The water is heated as it circulates near magma, the molten rock that lies just beneath the ocean floor. As the hot water spills

Huge red worms reach out from protective white tubes (left). The color of the worms comes from the same substance that makes human blood red. Some worms reach 12 feet (4 m) in length. They live in thick, spaghetti-like clumps near ocean-bottom hot springs.
N.G.S. PHOTOGRAPHER EMORY KRISTOF

Aboard the research vessel Melville *(right), John Favuzzi, on the left, and Joel Edelman assist biologist Alissa J. Arp of the Scripps Institution of Oceanography. They are sliding a tube worm out of its casing. The worm lived at a depth of 8,500 feet (2,591 m) in the Pacific Ocean.*

Mother ship Lulu *releases the tiny red submarine* Alvin *(below). Snorkelers jump off* Alvin *after removing lines tying it to* Lulu. *Repeated trips to the deep by* Alvin *produced startling photographs and other scientific information about unusual life growing around ocean-bottom vents. Dr. Robert Ballard, of the Woods Hole Oceanographic Institution, Woods Hole, Massachusetts, directed the work.*

HENRY GROSKINSKY

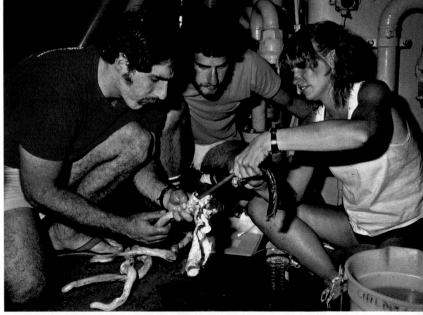

out, it mixes with the cold water of the deep ocean. The resulting lukewarm bath supports many kinds of life.

Creatures live near the vents because of the rich chemicals that spurt out of the vents. The chemical food supply for the bacteria is enormous. These tiny creatures, in turn, become food for tube worms, clams, mussels, and other life forms surrounding the vents.

The seafloor chimneys are called "black smokers." They shoot out superhot jets of mineral-rich water that resemble smoke. The "smoke" mixes with the ocean water. The building up, crumbling, and toppling of the chimneys leaves particles on the seafloor.

The deposits of iron, copper, zinc, sulfur, manganese, silver, and other minerals that come from the "black smokers" may turn out to be a valuable resource for people one day.

Researchers think that other ocean rift oases will be discovered—along with other surprises from the world without sun.

Minerals from the ocean bottom fill Dr. Ballard's hand (above). Specimens like this fragment from a "black smoker" help scientists pinpoint the source of chemicals and minerals in seawater. Now they know that much of the material shoots out from the ocean floor. Bacteria feed on chemicals. They are in turn eaten by such life forms as mussels, clams, and crabs seen in the large picture (right).

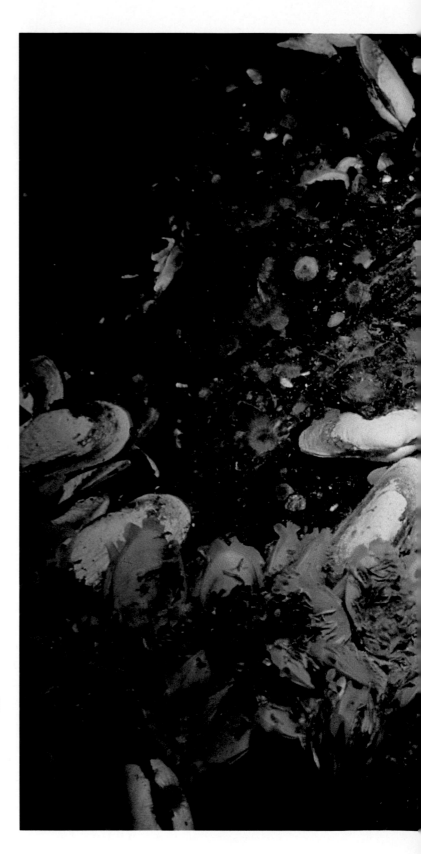

31

UNDERSEA SCHOOL

As scientists explore the depths of the sea and discover new life, they continue to study the mysteries of familiar forms of life. They ask, for instance, why fish swim in schools.

Scientists think swimming in schools protects fish from enemies. Watch a school of fish swimming sometime and you'll see why. It's hard to single out one member of the group and catch it.

If you have ever watched minnows in a pond swimming back and forth, all moving together like members of a well-trained water ballet, you may have wondered *how* they do it.

For many years, scientists thought that fish relied mostly on their vision to know when to dart and turn. Recent studies have shown that they use another method, too. A fish has "lateral lines," sense organs that run the length of its body along both sides. Special cells in these lines can sense tiny changes in the pressure and current of the water. These cells pick up such signals and help the fish maintain its position in the school.

In a large school, no individual fish acts as a leader. All the fish use their eyes and their lateral lines either to start new action or simply to keep their places in the underwater ballet. Each fish adjusts its speed and direction as the group constantly wheels, turns, breaks apart, and comes together again.

A school of fish called glassy sweepers swerves around a coral reef in the Red Sea. For years, scientists have studied such schools to find out how individual fish are able to turn and dart to keep up with the group.

32

CHAPTER 3

LOST WORLDS

Some of the world's most amazing mysteries center on ancient civilizations. What long-forgotten people carved stone statues found today in far-off tropical forests? Who built lost cities on lone mountaintops? Who cut huge drawings into the bare earth? The people are gone, but they left behind many clues for archaeologists to study.

Archaeologists are scientists who are trained to recognize and explain clues from past civilizations.

Archaeologists are busy studying the stone figures shown here. Hundreds of statues like these hide in the wooded mountains of Colombia, a country in South America. Much remains to be learned about the people who carved the statues. How did they live? What did they believe? Where did they go?

In this chapter, guided by archaeologists, you will explore other lost worlds. You'll look at the clues left behind and let them speak for the people who are gone.

This moss-covered statue may be 1,500 years old (above). It stands in the San Agustín region of Colombia, in South America.
LOREN McINTYRE

A figure with frightening fangs guards a forest trail (right). More than 300 such statues dot this part of Colombia.
M.J. ADAMS/OXFORD SCIENTIFIC FILMS

SILENCE OF CENTURIES

Far out in the Pacific Ocean, off the coast of South America, lies a small, bare island. In 1722, a Dutch explorer landed there on Easter Sunday and named it Easter Island.

If you visited the island by boat, you would notice something strange about it even before you reached the shore. Along the beaches, atop seaside cliffs, and in the meadows stand mysterious stone figures. They have big heads, and those along the coast look inland. Some wear hatlike topknots carved from huge stone blocks. Some statues are small—about three feet (1 m) tall or less. Others are huge and

GEORG GERSTER

Like silent soldiers, stone figures stand guard on lonely Easter Island (above). When a Dutch explorer landed on the remote Pacific island in 1722, he was amazed to find hundreds of statues like these.

A stone topknot caps a huge head (right). Islanders once held religious ceremonies on the level area in front of the figure. More statues stand on a nearby beach.

36

37

would tower over you if you stood beside them. What are these stone figures, and where did they come from?

Local legends say that, long ago, people arrived by boat, settled on the island, and started carving the statues to honor their ancestors. Scientists who have studied the site think that is what did happen. But why did the islanders stop carving the statues? It appears that the carving suddenly stopped sometime in the 17th century. Early explorers found many unfinished statues on the hillsides. Stone tools lay around them, as if the carvers had put them down and walked away.

As the people who settled the island grew more and more numerous, trouble started. Land became scarce, and people were crowded. A civil war began. Many people were killed, and many of the stone statues that rival groups used in their religious ceremonies were knocked to the ground, faces in the dirt.

The strange statues, some of which are hundreds of years old, could tell us a lot—but they are not talking.

N.G.S. PHOTOGRAPHER JAMES P. BLAIR

Time has almost worn away the body and face of this statue (below). Centuries ago, when it was new, its features were smooth. Islanders carved it from soft volcanic rock, using tools made of harder stone.

Human figure gives an idea of the size of this statue (above). Early islanders carved it from the dark volcanic stone in the background. For years, the statue stood buried to its shoulders.

Unfinished figures, partly carved from a hillside, sleep forever in their stone bunks (left). When visitors to the island discovered this quarry, they found stone tools scattered on the ground near the statues. Apparently, the carvers suddenly gave up their task and abandoned the half-completed statues.

CITY IN THE CLOUDS

In 1911, an explorer named Hiram Bingham climbed high in the Andes, a chain of mountains in South America. One afternoon, a Peruvian Indian boy led the explorer up a rough trail that ended in an area between two bare mountain peaks.

"The sight held me spellbound," Bingham wrote later. There were stairways, temples, houses, and streets. All were nearly buried under hundreds of years of plant growth. The place was called Machu Picchu (MAH-chew PEA-chew) after one of the nearby mountain peaks. The name means "old mountain." The following year, backed by research grants from the National Geographic Society and Yale University, Bingham returned and began to dig out the city.

Archaeologists have learned that the Inca (ING-kuh) people built Machu Picchu some five centuries ago. Hundreds of people lived in the city. It was an important religious center. It was also a fortress, located so high in the mountains that it would be hard to attack.

Spanish invaders destroyed many other cities of the Inca people. But they never reached Machu Picchu. In time, however, the city high in the clouds became deserted. Today, no crops grow in the terraced fields. No water flows in the fountains. Visitors from everywhere come to marvel at Machu Picchu.

Stone houses crowd steep, narrow streets high in South America's mountains (above). This is Machu Picchu (MAH-chew PEA-chew), where Incas once lived.

When an Indian boy led explorer Hiram Bingham to Machu Picchu in 1911, trees covered the site. This 1912 picture (below) shows the ruins partly cleared.

41

If you give a crayon to a little child, the child will probably draw a picture. The picture may be just a couple of lines, but it means something to the child.

People have always loved to draw, from hunters who recorded on cave walls pictures of the animals they saw around them to European artists who painted visions of heaven and earth on the ceilings of churches. Some people—in places around the world—have drawn pictures right on the ground.

In Peru, more than 1,500 years ago, the Nazca people made lines by removing the top dark layer of rocks from dry plains and mountainsides. The sandy layer below, being lighter

MARION MORRISON

Peruvian schoolchildren (above) draw a line by removing the top layer of dark stone to expose the lighter ground beneath. Almost 2,000 years ago, their ancestors made large drawings the same way.

Seen from the air, lines made centuries ago form the shape of an enormous hummingbird (right). No one knows why the Nazca people made such drawings.

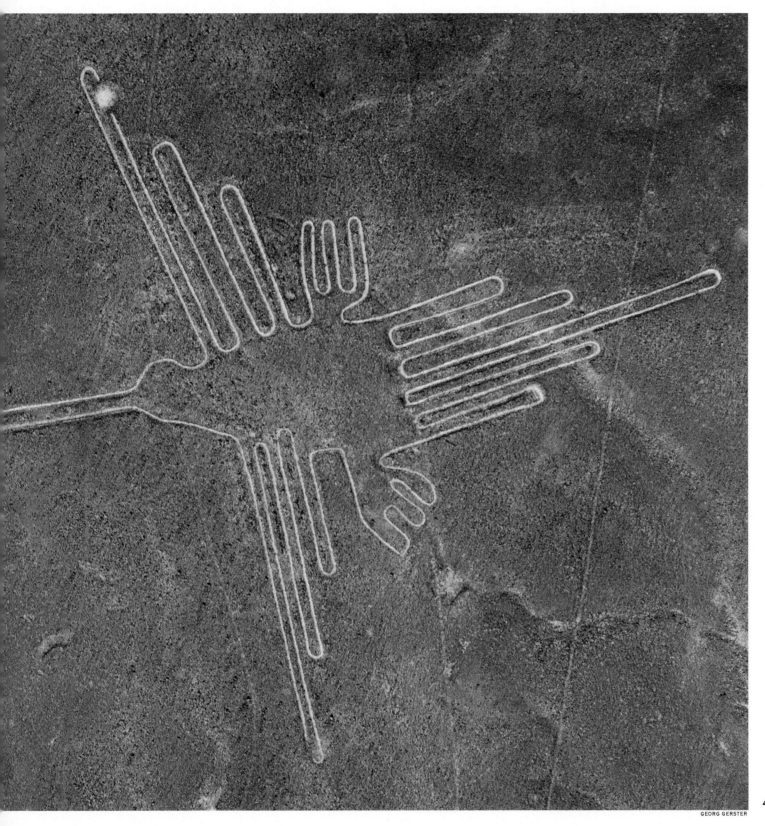

43

in color, showed up clearly. The people drew long, straight lines. They also drew pictures of birds and whales, a spider and a monkey.

The strangest thing is that the drawings are so big they can be fully appreciated only if seen from high above. The Nazca artists never saw their work the way people can see it today—from the air.

The world still wonders what the drawings were for. Perhaps Nazcas drew them for their gods in the sky to look down on.

Other people in other places also shaped huge pictures on the ground. In England, ancient Celts made a horse figure by cutting into the earth to expose white chalk below the surface. In Ohio, Indians piled earth in a long, curving line that looks like a large snake.

Many of the mysteries of earth art remain. It's clear, though, that we can see these figures better today, from airplanes, than the artists themselves ever could.

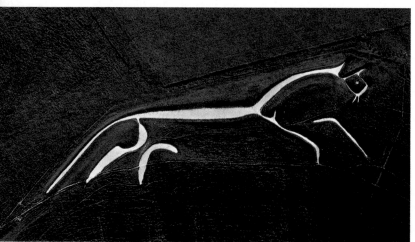

People carved a galloping horse into a chalky hillside in England about 2,000 years ago (above). The horse is visible on clear days from 20 miles (32 km) away.

American Indians made the likeness of a snake by piling earth in a curving line (right). The oval shape on the far right may represent an egg the snake is eating.

44

*Visitors mount steep steps to reach a temple atop a pyramid in Palenque (pah-*LENG*-kay), a ruined city in Mexico 13 centuries old.*

46

PYRAMIDS, TEMPLES, AND TOMBS

We think of tall buildings as modern developments. We watch skyscrapers go up, quickly built by cranes, concrete mixers, and other special construction equipment.

But people in ancient times built tall, dazzling buildings also. And they did it using simple tools and a sure knowledge of engineering. Some of their structures took years to build.

In the dense jungles of southern Mexico and Central America, explorers have discovered towering pyramids built by a people called the Maya (MY-yuh). Grand palaces once housed rulers and their families. Pyramids covered the tombs of kings. Temples rose high above the countryside, gleaming with red or blue paint. Long ago, however, the Maya civilization began to break apart. People left the magnificent cities and moved to small towns and villages. The jungle took over, burying even the largest buildings under vines and leaves.

Many Maya buildings wait to be discovered. Searchers have found some in recent times, and they know many more ruins still lie buried under jungle growth, waiting to be uncovered.

On the other side of the world, other ancient peoples also built huge structures. In Egypt and the Sudan (Continued on page 50)

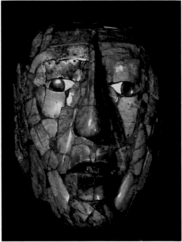

MUSEO NACIONAL DE ANTROPOLOGÍA, MEXICO CITY

Pieces of jade form a death mask (above) for Pacal, a Maya ruler buried in the Palenque pyramid.

Inside the pyramid, archaeologists made a spectacular discovery: the tomb of Pacal (left), a great king. For centuries, the tomb remained hidden at the bottom of a long stairwell filled with rocks.
GEORG GERSTER

47

Long ago, ancient architects designed this temple at El Tajín (tah-HEEN), near Veracruz, in Mexico. They built it so the windowlike squares create dramatic shadows, and they painted it red. At night, modern lighting and a red photographic filter serve to re-create the temple's original awesome appearance.
DAVID HISER

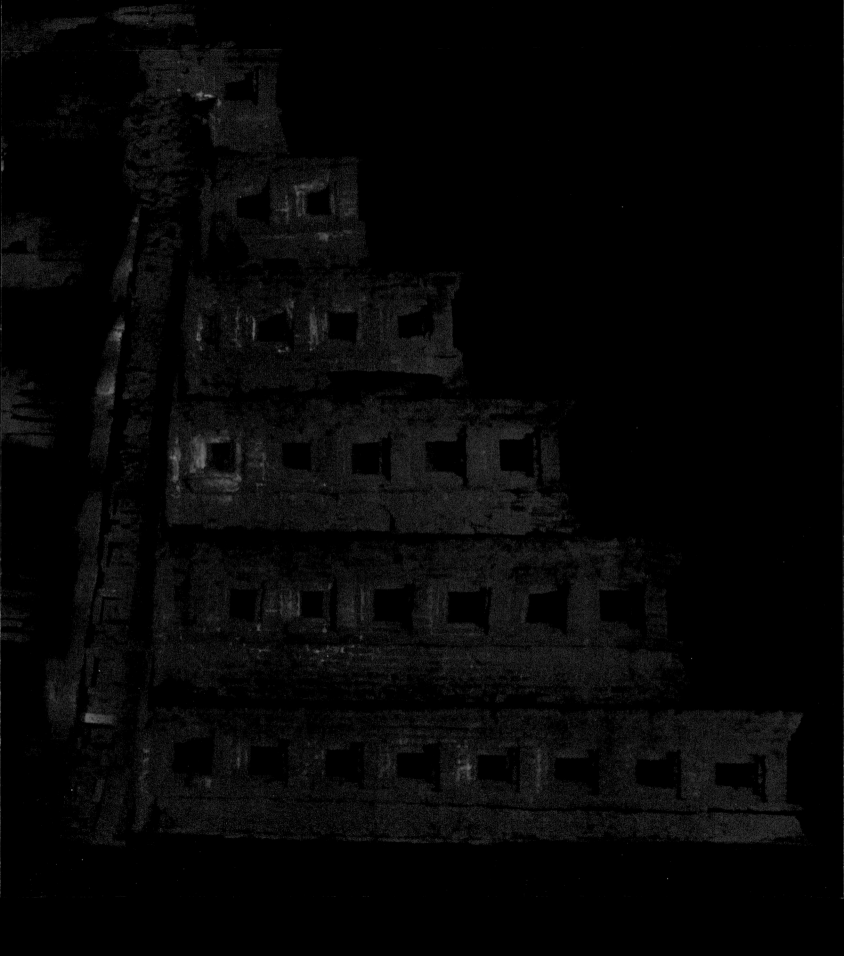

(*Continued from page 47*) in Africa, pyramids tower over the desert. For centuries, people have wondered about the civilizations that built the pyramids. How were these four-sided structures made and what were they used for? Archaeologists have found royal tombs beneath the pyramids in the Sudan. An ancient people called the Kushites built the pyramids as huge tombs for their kings.

Most archaeologists believe the famous pyramids of Egypt mark the tombs of pharaohs, ancient Egyptian rulers who were worshiped throughout the kingdom as gods.

The pyramids still stagger the imagination. They are marvels of engineering, built without the use of iron tools or even the wheel. Imagine how difficult it must have been almost 5,000 years ago to construct a 40-story-high pyramid whose four equal sides had to meet in an exact point at the very top. How did the ancient Egyptians do it? Lifelong students of the subject think they know. Their research tells us that part of the answer lies in the drawing below.

Crumbling pyramids (above) cover the graves of long-dead kings of Kush, who at one time conquered and ruled Egypt. Built more than 2,000 years ago, these pyramids cover underground burial chambers.

50

GEORG GERSTER

TOM PIX/PETER ARNOLD, INC.

This drawing (below) shows workmen preparing to drag a stone up an inclined plane toward a pyramid under construction in Egypt. Pouring water on the soil helps the huge stone slide more easily.

Pyramids mark the desert at Giza, in Egypt (above). Scientists believe they are the tombs of kings. The remaining mystery: Exactly how did people 5,000 years ago plan and build such perfect structures?

ROBERT E. HYNES

STONE AGE ASTRONOMY

An observatory is a place where scientists called astronomers study the movements of the sun, moon, stars, planets, and comets. If you have ever visited an observatory, you know that the most important piece of equipment there is a telescope. How else can you study the heavens, after all?

Actually, humans knew a great deal about the movements of the objects in the sky many centuries before the telescope was invented. In fact, some of the information we use today to identify stars comes from the ancient Babylonians and Greeks.

How did ancient people unravel mysteries of the sky? How did they know when an eclipse would happen, when the moon would be full, or when the constellation Great Bear would lie just above the horizon?

They knew simply by watching. They paid close attention to what went on in the sky. They watched the way the sun's position changed every day. And they remembered, or kept rough records from year to year and generation to generation.

Eventually, ancient astronomers began building structures to help them keep better track of sky events—and to predict when the

On summer's first day, the light of the rising sun glows through the pillars of Stonehenge, in England (below). Archaeologists believe that priests once used the circle of standing stones to study the heavens.

GEORG GERSTER

52

Working without metal tools, ancient people shape the huge slabs for Stonehenge in this painting (above). Groups of men raise stones off the ground by rolling logs under them. Using fire for heat, then water to cool the stone quickly, they weaken the slabs along a desired line. In the foreground, a team repeatedly drops round rocks on a line to square off the end of a huge slab.

How did workmen at Stonehenge get the huge pillars to stand up? In the painting (left), an artist shows how it might have been done. First, workers inched the stone off a sled of logs until it dropped into a waiting hole. Then workmen built a structure called a crib to support it. Here, using long poles, they prepare to tilt the 50-ton (45-t) slab into an upright position.

53

events might happen again. Such structures served as observatories, just as do the ones today that have telescopes.

Many people believe that Stonehenge, in southern England, is a huge, circular observatory. People 4,000 or more years ago carefully placed large stones on end in such a way that they lined up with points on the horizon. These points were where the sun rose and set on certain days of the year. Important days were the equinoxes, the two times each year when day and night are of equal length.

Elsewhere in the British Isles—and in other parts of Europe—people built similar circles of standing stones. On the Orkney Islands, off the coast of Scotland, the Ring of Brogar may also have been used as a kind of observatory. Its stones may have helped the people keep track of the movement of the moon.

At other places and times, people figured out similar things about movements in the sky. In what is now New Mexico, ancient Indians called the Anasazi (ah-nuh-SAH-zee) carved a spiral on a cliff face that allowed them to keep track of the sun's position. On the summer solstice, the first day of summer—

In Scotland, the rising sun shines through the Ring of Brogar (above). Like Stonehenge, the ring may have been used by people thousands of years ago to help predict movements of the sun and the moon.

Scientists have studied the Ring of Brogar from the air (right) to try to figure out how ancient astronomers used it. A Scottish engineer made charts and measurements of the ring, and decided that it could have been used to predict eclipses of the moon.

54

a time when many ancient peoples conducted religious ceremonies—a "sun dagger" divides the spiral exactly in half. Sunlight shining between slabs of rock forms the dagger.

Many astronomers of today have become interested in how well ancient peoples understood what happens in the sky. Recently, scientists have been using modern equipment to take measurements at ancient sites in North and South America to find out more about how our ancestors kept track of time. These scholars use both archaeology and astronomy to unlock secrets of the past.

GEORG GERSTER

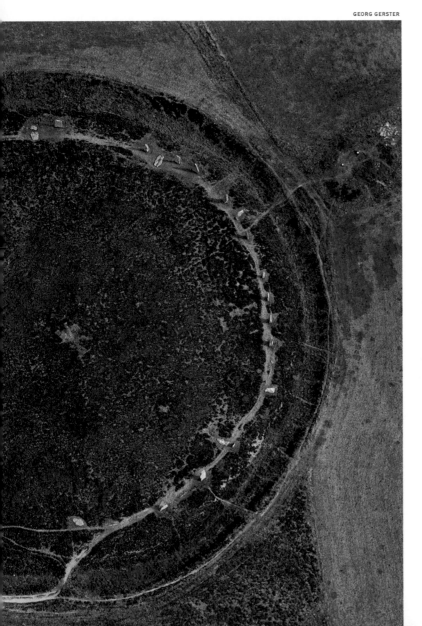

DAVID BRILL

On the first day of summer, sunlight strikes through the center of a spiral carved on a cliff face in New Mexico. Indians worked out this device to signal the summer solstice (SAHL-stuss). Ancient civilizations throughout the world used such "stone clocks" the way we use watches and calendars.

55

MESSAGES FROM THE PAST

It's exciting to see signs left behind by ancient people—like the amazing wall art shown on these pages.

When you look at the drawings, you're seeing messages from people you can never talk with. You will never be able to read their writings, either, because they did not have any written language.

But through their art, you learn what kinds of things interested early American Indians who made the pictures on these pages. You'd have to say animals. This suggests that the artists were hunters, and that they were interested in the natural world. But what about those footprints, or the odd squiggly lines?

All over the world, from a cave with mud-coated walls in Tennessee to limestone caves in France, people who once lived on this planet left messages that we still puzzle over. Maybe someday you can solve some of them.

All the news that's fit to carve. At Utah's Newspaper Rock State Historical Monument (left), modern eyes can look at messages from the past. Long ago, artists made drawings to tell stories of hunting adventures. Many drawings represent animals and are easy to understand. Others—like the wagon wheel shape—remain mysteries that we may never unravel.

GARY LADD   BILL DEANE (ABOVE AND BELOW)

Drawings made centuries ago on the mud walls of a cave in Tennessee (above) are still as clear as if the Indian artists had just walked away. Here, anthropologist Charles Faulkner, of the University of Tennessee, examines the drawings, recently discovered by people exploring the cave for fun.

An Indian artist used a stick or a fingertip to draw this little owl (left). The drawing dates from before the 16th century.

57

CHAPTER 4

OUT OF THIS WORLD

Have you ever spent an evening looking up at the stars? If so, you have probably thought about how huge the region beyond our planet must be.

It's hard to imagine the size of the universe. Astronomers measure space distances in units called light-years. A light-year is the distance light travels through space in one year. It's six *trillion* miles—a 6 with 12 zeros after it (9.7 trillion km). The North Star is 4,080 trillion miles (6,566 trillion km) away. The light you see actually left the star 680 years ago! Some of the stars astronomers study are so far away that their light takes *billions* of years to reach us.

Ancient people who gazed up at the heavens found many mysteries there. As scientists developed powerful telescopes, they explained some of the old mysteries. But they also discovered new ones, such as black holes. Most of the universe remains a seemingly endless series of riddles that continue to challenge scientists.

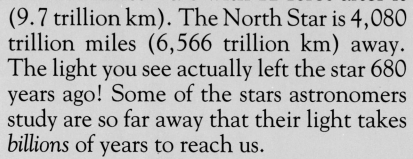

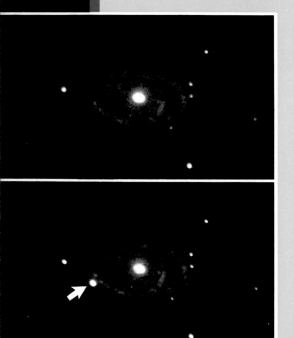

The M 100 galaxy looked like this (top) before a star exploded (arrow, bottom). Such an explosion is called a supernova.
BEN MAYER

Gases from a 20,000-year-old supernova curve across the sky (right). A supernova may have helped to create our solar system.
© CALIFORNIA INSTITUTE OF TECHNOLOGY 1959

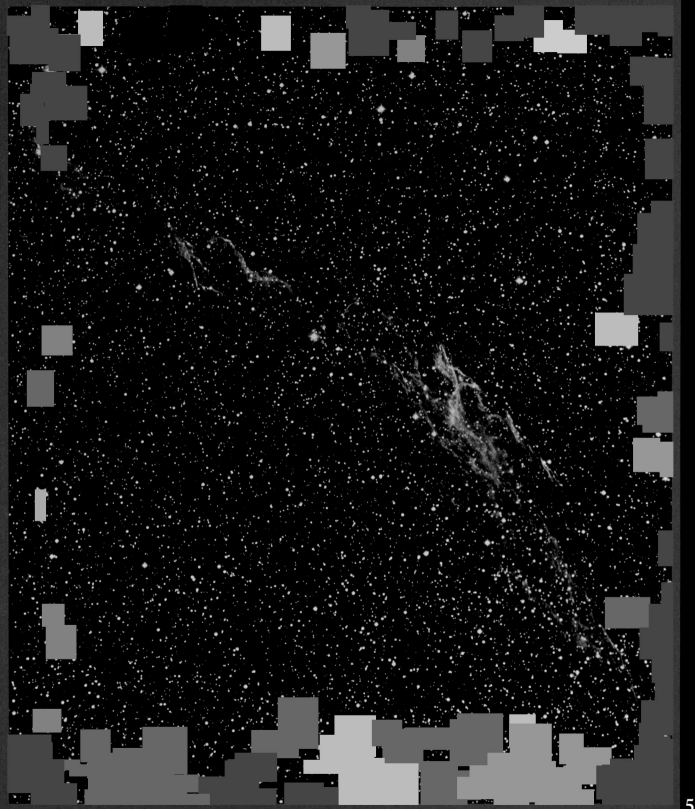

BLACK HOLES

Like living things on earth, stars have life cycles. All are born, shine for a while, and eventually go out. Astronomers believe stars form in clouds of gases and dust. What happens to them after that depends mostly on their mass.

Mass is the amount of material an object contains. If a small star contains more material than a large star, the small star is more massive than the large one. Stars shine because they burn some of their mass as fuel. The most massive stars burn fuel fastest. They have the shortest lives.

The core, or center, of the star serves as its furnace. As a star begins to run out of fuel, its core begins to collapse. Gravity, the same force that holds you on earth, holds the star together. Gravity squeezes the material in the core more and more tightly together.

Have you ever taken a piece of bread and squished it with your fingers until it formed a ball? You didn't change the amount of material in the bread, but you did shrink the amount of space the material occupied. The same mass became more densely packed.

Something similar happens to the collapsing core of a cooling star. It becomes more dense and, as it does, its gravity becomes stronger. A cosmic tug-of-war takes place within the star. As the gases in its core heat up, they expand. At the same time, gravity tries to pull the gases together. In stars like our sun, the tug-of-war goes on for a long time. The star gives off light or other signals for several billion years. Astronomers say our sun is

BLACK HOLE

SWIRLING GASES

four and a half billion years old. They expect it to shine for at least five billion more.

A much more massive star doesn't live that long. Its core becomes *very* dense. The strong gravity pulls in the star's remaining gases. Not even light can escape. Nothing remains that you can see with your eyes or with a normal telescope. But something is still out there—something most scientists call a black hole.

What happens to materials that are pulled into black holes? That's a mystery scientists are trying to solve. You don't have to worry about disappearing into a black hole because none have been detected near earth. The closest one is about 8,000 light-years away!

60

GIANT STAR

DON DIXON

Could the power of a black hole's gravity help people explore our galaxy one day? Maybe. Scientists have already used the gravity of the planet Jupiter to give the Voyager and Pioneer space probes a boost. In the painting below, a probe passes Jupiter. The planet's gravitational field grabs the probe and flings it farther into space. Perhaps a black hole could be used in a similar way. Its gravity could make a spaceship travel farther, faster than the ship could travel on its own (bottom). Of course, the spaceship couldn't get too close to the black hole. If it did, it would be sucked in.

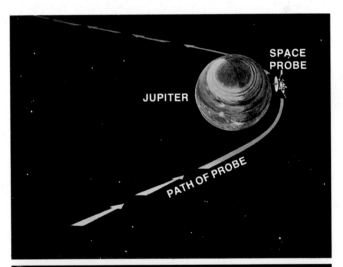

JUPITER

SPACE PROBE

PATH OF PROBE

The painting above shows what astronomers think a black hole might be like. This one is about 8,000 light-years away, in the constellation Cygnus. Here, the black hole and a giant star circle each other. Gases from the star swirl around the hole. Gases that get too close are pulled in by the black hole's incredibly strong gravity. Some of the swirling gases give off powerful X rays. Certain scientific instruments can detect the rays and measure their strength. They provide clues to the locations of black holes. The holes themselves are invisible. Scientists discovered evidence of this one in 1965 with special equipment aboard a rocket.

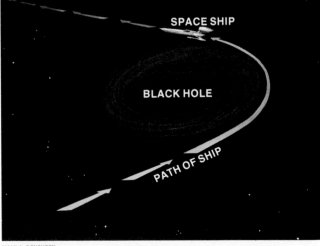

SPACE SHIP

BLACK HOLE

PATH OF SHIP

SALLY J. BENSUSEN

61

RACING THROUGH SPACE

Chances are you've seen *The Empire Strikes Back,* one of the most popular space movies ever made. You've watched Han Solo rev up his spaceship and zoom through the universe as if it were the size of your backyard. In real life, such travel may never be possible. If we could travel at the speed of light, we could visit some of the closest stars. But by the time a ship could reach the nearest galaxy, nearly two million years would have passed on earth!

In The Empire Strikes Back, *Han Solo, Princess Leia, See-Threepio, and Chewbacca take the spaceship* Millennium Falcon *to distant parts of the universe (above). This kind of space travel is still a dream. It may one day become reality within our solar system, but probably not to faraway galaxies.*

Pursued by enemy spaceships, the Millennium Falcon *weaves and dodges through a field of asteroids. Solo and his quick-thinking crew manage to avoid both the enemy guns and the asteroids.*

63

SIGNALING STARS

In 1967, some scientists in England received a mysterious "message" from space. They were using a radio telescope—an instrument that picks up distant radio waves. The scientists detected signals coming from a faraway object. The signals came at such regular intervals that, at first, the scientists wondered if another civilization could be sending them. They nicknamed the source of the radio beams LGM, for "Little Green Men."

As the scientists gathered more information, they decided that the signals came from a new kind of star. They called it a pulsar, because its signals were regular, like the pulse in your wrist. Scientists think a pulsar forms when a massive star explodes as a supernova. The core of the star may collapse into a small, but very massive and rapidly spinning star.

Most stars have magnetic fields, just as the earth has. When a collapsing star shrinks, its magnetic field grows stronger. Electrically charged particles from gases around the star get caught in the magnetic field. As these particles spin with the star, they give off signals.

At first the star has so much energy that it sends out both light waves and radio waves. The spinning motion makes the waves appear and disappear, just as the rotating beam in a lighthouse appears to flash off and on.

Over thousands of years, the spinning pulsar gradually loses energy. It slows down and sends out only radio waves. They pulse more and more slowly. After about ten million years, the star stops broadcasting. Astronomers think that our galaxy contains at least one million active pulsars and another *thousand million* silent ones.

Although pulsars form when certain massive stars explode, there seem to be more pulsars than massive star explosions. Where did the other signaling stars come from? That's a question scientists are trying to answer.

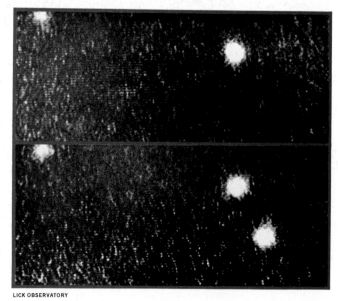

LICK OBSERVATORY

Pulsar birthplace. The Crab Nebula (right) appeared in the sky after a supernova. Skywatchers saw and recorded the explosion in 1054. The word nebula means "mist" or "cloud." Gases in this nebula came from the exploding star. The explosion also left something else behind—a small, very dense star (arrow). It was formed by the collapse of the giant star's core. The small star is a young, energetic pulsar. As it spins, it sends out regular bursts of energy in the form of radio waves and light waves.

© CALIFORNIA INSTITUTE OF TECHNOLOGY 1959

Two photographs show the Crab pulsar at different times (left). In the top picture, you see two bright stars. In the bottom picture, you see three. The third star is the rapidly spinning pulsar. Its light appears to wink off and on as the pulsar spins. Both photographs are closer views of the area inside the rectangle (right).

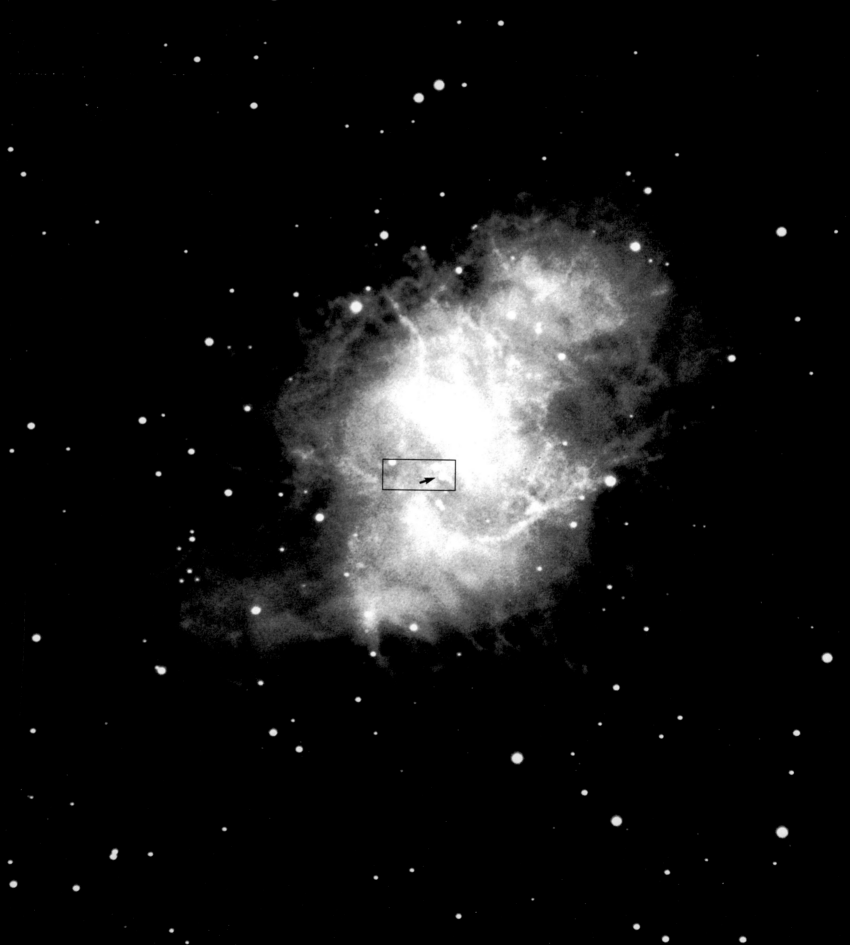

PINT-SIZE PLANETS

If a cosmic highway department ever put up solar system road signs, the area between Mars and Jupiter would be loaded with warnings: "Watch out for speeding asteroids!"

Asteroids are odd-shaped chunks of rock and metal that orbit the sun. They are sometimes called minor planets. Astronomers have identified more than two thousand asteroids and think hundreds of thousands may be whirling around in our solar system. Occasionally, asteroids crash into each other. The collisions give them odd shapes and scarred surfaces. The largest asteroid ever measured is about as broad as Texas. The smallest may be less than a half mile (1 km) across.

Most asteroids travel in a wide band between Mars and Jupiter. This belt is a kind of dividing line in the solar system. Planets inside the belt—Mercury, Venus, Earth, and Mars—are rocky objects. The four large planets outside the belt—Jupiter, Saturn, Uranus, and Neptune—are made up mostly of gases.

Where did asteroids come from? Scientists once thought that they formed when a large planet between Mars and Jupiter exploded. Now astronomers doubt this theory. There simply isn't enough solid material out there to make a large planet. If you put all the known asteroids together, you'd get an object smaller than the earth's moon! Most astronomers now believe the pint-size planets are rubble left over from the time the solar system formed more than four and a half billion years ago. You could compare them to the chunks of brick and wood you sometimes see left over at construction sites. Occasionally, pieces of asteroids reach the earth. When they do, they are called by another name—meteorites.

SALLY J. BENSUSEN

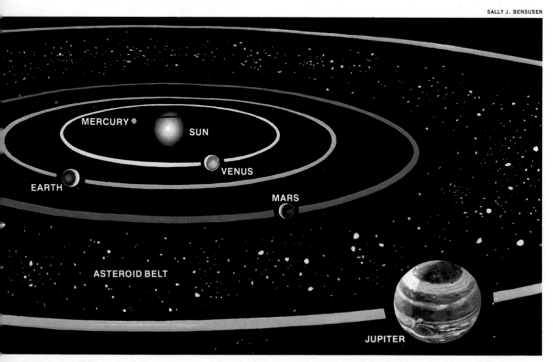

Asteroids form a belt between Mars and Jupiter (left). If you traveled outward from the sun in a spacecraft, you would pass Mercury, Venus, Earth, and Mars. Then you might have to do some tricky navigating to move through the asteroid belt and reach Jupiter. This painting shows the order of these planets, but not their relative sizes.

Phobos, one of the two moons of Mars (right), may have been an asteroid captured by the gravity of Mars and pulled into orbit around the planet. Scientists believe Deimos, the other moon of Mars, may have been an asteroid, too.

NASA

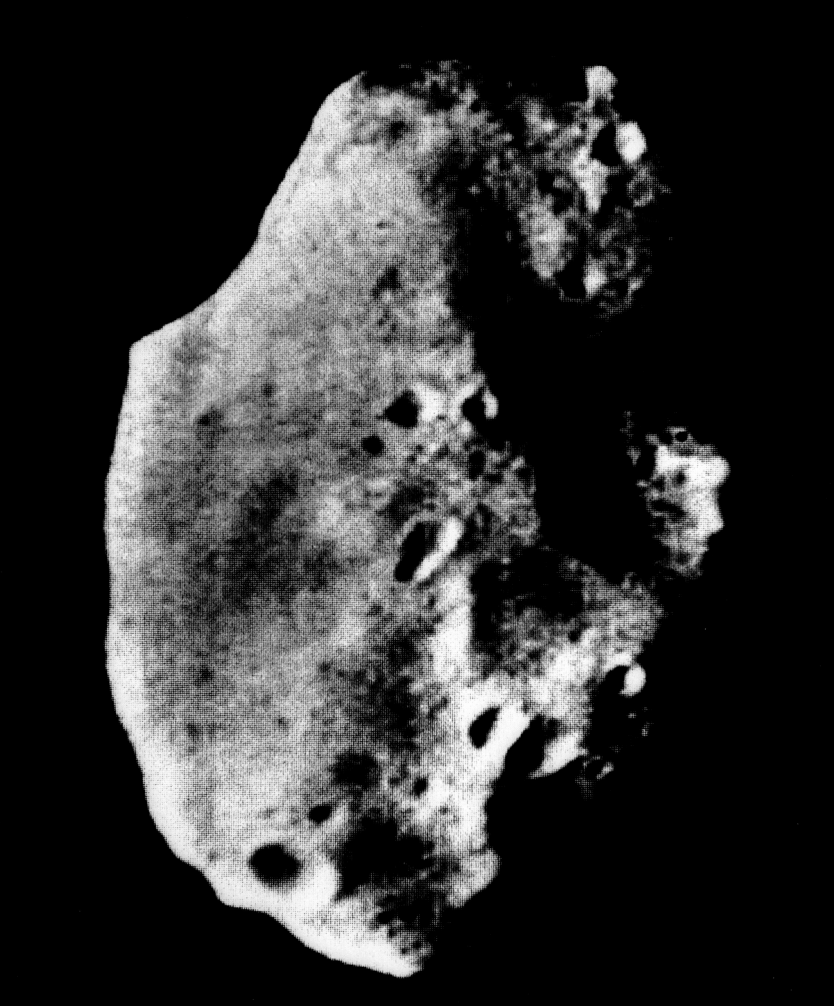

VISITORS FROM SPACE

It's late at night, and you're lying in a lawn chair looking at the stars. Suddenly a streak of light flashes across the sky. "I saw a shooting star!" you shout.

Actually, what you saw was not a star. It was a meteor, the trail of light produced by a piece of cosmic material hurtling through our atmosphere. That material is called a meteoroid. It may once have been part of an asteroid, and it probably has been traveling for millions, or even billions, of years. The meteoroid zoomed into the earth's atmosphere at about 60,000 miles an hour (96,558 km/h). Friction caused by the atmosphere heated the meteoroid's outer layer, causing it to glow.

Meteoroids fall into our atmosphere all the time. Most are no larger than a grain of sand. They are destroyed on their fiery trip and never reach the earth. Occasionally larger ones, the size of small rocks, survive. When they land, they are called meteorites. Every year, people discover a few of these meteorites and put them on exhibit in museums. Once in many thousands of years, a giant meteorite falls and blasts a crater like those shown here.

Astronomers believe that meteoroids, asteroids, and comets have changed very little since the beginning of the solar system. They

GEORG GERSTER (ABOVE AND RIGHT)

Space scars. Scientists think a meteorite as big as a railroad flatcar slammed into what is now the Arizona desert more than 20,000 years ago. It left a hole about four-fifths of a mile (1 km) across (above). That hole is now called Meteor Crater. In Australia, Gosses Bluff (right) marks the spot where scientists believe a meteorite crashed about 130 million years ago. The inner rim of this crater measures about 3 miles (5 km) across. Scientists think the original crater was larger. Rain and wind have worn most of it away.

68

Polished and treated with acid, a piece of a meteorite found in Canada shows a crisscross pattern (above). It tells experts that this is an iron meteorite. Scientists divide meteorites into three groups. Stony meteorites are mostly rock. Stony-iron meteorites are a mixture of rock and metal. Iron meteorites are mostly metal.

Straight streaks of light mark the paths of meteoroids (above). Meteoroids that travel in groups probably come from comets. The curved lines are star tracks. While the camera shutter was left open for this picture, the earth's rotation made the stars appear to move. 69

think all these objects were formed during the same period as the sun and the planets.

Scientists believe most comets stay in the outer reaches of the solar system. Some, however, pass close to the sun from time to time. They may come very near the earth.

That's what may have happened in 1908 near Tunguska, a remote part of Siberia, in the Soviet Union. People living nearby saw a brilliant light in the sky. Then they heard a tremendous explosion. The blast destroyed a wooded area nearly as large as Rhode Island.

For years, people wondered about the cause of the blast. Some believed it was a meteorite. But why didn't it leave a crater? Other people suggested that it was an exploding spaceship. But no evidence of a spaceship was found. Many astronomers now believe a small comet caused the destruction. As the comet entered the earth's atmosphere, it blew apart. Small bits fell to earth, leaving no crater. Heat waves and shock waves spread, like ripples from a stone hitting water. The waves flattened and burned trees, killed wildlife—and left people puzzling over what had occurred.

Trees fell like toothpicks when a gigantic explosion rocked Tunguska, a wilderness area in the central part of the Soviet Union. The blast occurred in 1908. For years, its cause puzzled and challenged scientists. Most experts now believe a comet caused the blast.

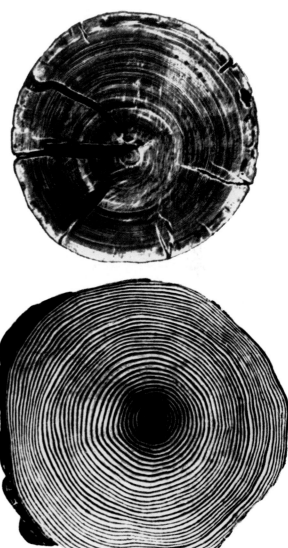

The top cross section came from a tree killed by the explosion. Its growth rings are close together. The other section came from a tree that grew after the blast. Its rings are farther apart—a sign of faster growth. Some people suggest that radiation from an exploding spaceship might have caused the fast growth. Most experts, however, believe it resulted from more growing room in the wasted area. 71

SPEEDING SNOWBALLS

Comets don't swoop by the earth often—but when they do they cause a lot of excitement! Their name comes from a Greek word meaning "long-haired."

That's a good description. As a comet nears the sun, gases and dust stream out from it, forming a tail. The tail looks somewhat like long hair blowing in the breeze.

Not so long ago, comets terrified people. They believed that a comet was a sure sign of disaster. As recently as 1910, some people thought the appearance of Halley's (HAL-leez) comet meant the end of the world was near.

Halley's comet reappears every 76 years or so. It will be closest to the sun—and to the earth—in 1986. With the unaided eye, you may not see much more than a fuzzy patch in the sky. Scientists will use powerful telescopes to study the comet. Some countries will launch space probes to send back information.

Scientists believe the probes will confirm the theory that comets are made up of ice, dust, and gases. One astronomer calls them "dirty snowballs." Astronomers believe the snowballs come from a cloud called the Oort cloud. It is near the outer limits of our solar system. The cloud contains millions of small clumps of ice and dust. Each clump is the nucleus, or center, of a comet.

Every now and then, the gravity of a passing star pulls a dirty snowball out of the cloud. When that happens, the snowball may start

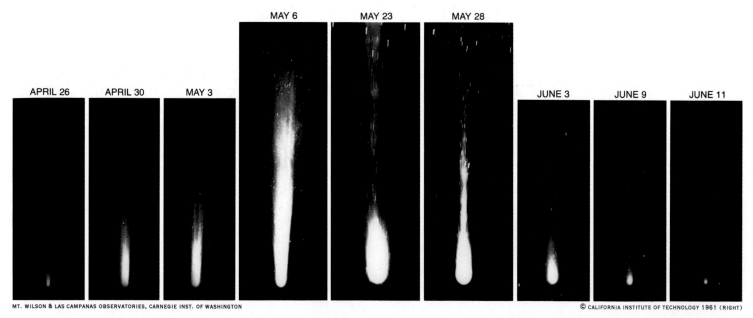

MAY 6   MAY 23   MAY 28

APRIL 26   APRIL 30   MAY 3   JUNE 3   JUNE 9   JUNE 11

MT. WILSON & LAS CAMPANAS OBSERVATORIES, CARNEGIE INST. OF WASHINGTON © CALIFORNIA INSTITUTE OF TECHNOLOGY 1961 (RIGHT)

Photographs made in 1910 show Halley's comet (above). In May, when the comet was closest to the earth, observers got a good look at its tail. In April and June, the tail seemed smaller because of the position of the comet in relation to the earth.

An astronomer discovered Comet Humason (right) in 1961, in the area between Mars and Jupiter. Bluish gases form a short tail. This comet never came close to the earth. It won't be visible again for almost 3,000 years. The streaks of light are star tracks.

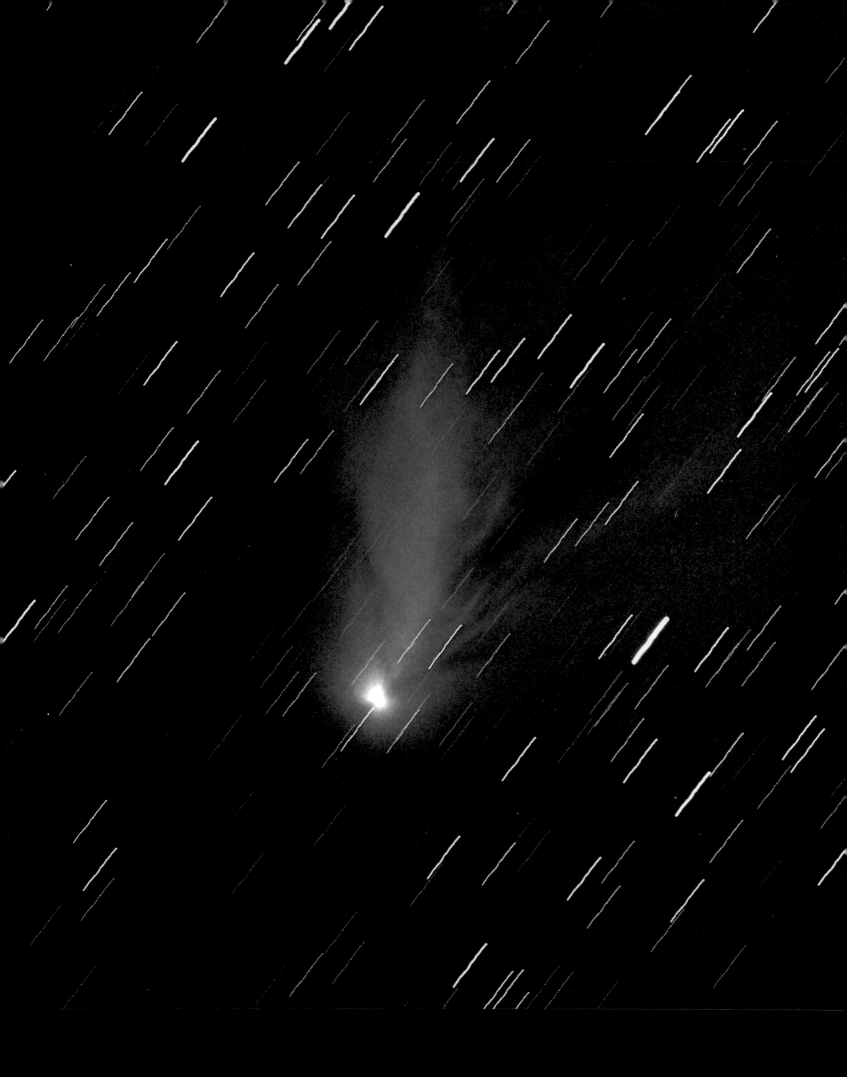

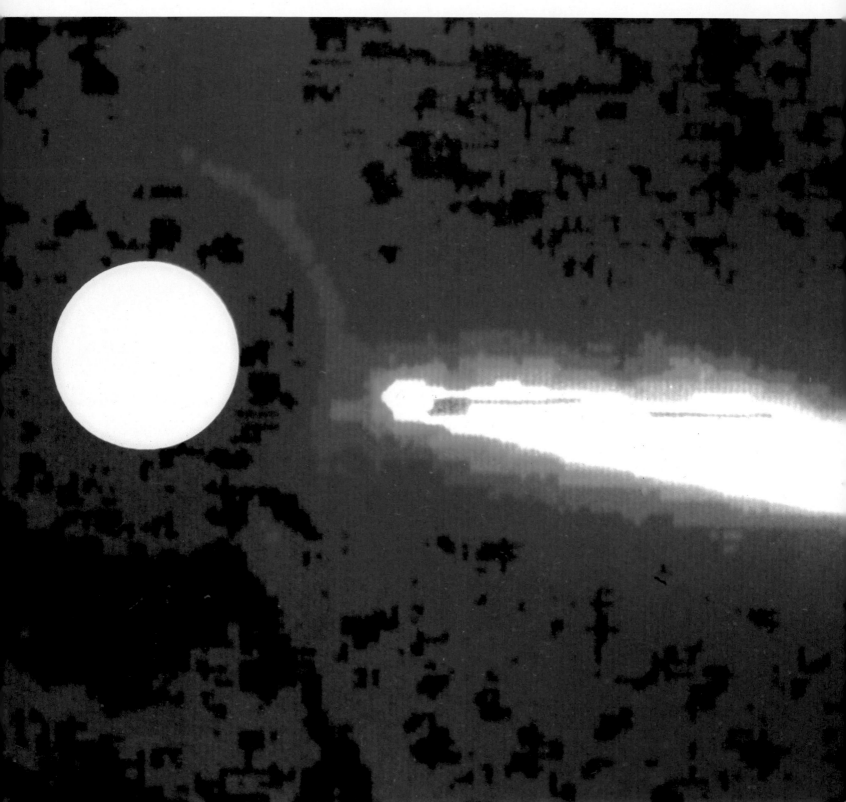

on a long journey toward the sun. As the snowball approaches the sun, some of its ice vaporizes. It turns directly into gases without becoming liquid, just as dry ice does. Gases soon surround the nucleus. They form the comet's head, or coma. As the comet comes closer to the sun, some gases may stream out behind it, forming a tail. Dust particles freed from the ice may form a second tail.

Astronomers spot about two dozen comets each year with their telescopes. About half of these are "new" comets. Nobody has recorded their appearance before. The orbits of some comets bring them so close to the sun that they burn up. Others, affected by the gravity of large planets in our solar system, continue to orbit the sun fairly regularly.

Halley's is such a comet. It takes its name from Edmund Halley, a British astronomer. He suggested that what people thought were different comets were really regular reappearances of the same comet. He announced his theory around 1700. He predicted that the comet would reappear in 1758—and he was right. If you watch Halley's comet in 1986, you'll be looking at the same speeding snowball that passed over Rome in 87 B.C., when Julius Caesar was only 13 years old. And you may wonder who'll be looking at the comet in 2061 when it zooms by our planet again.

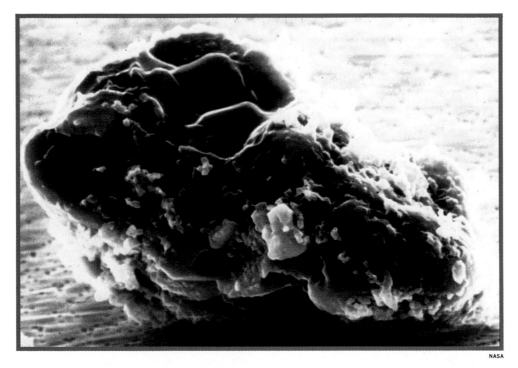

NASA

Fiery death. In this photograph made by a satellite, a comet heads straight for the sun (left). Once there, it will become part of the glowing ball. Until this photograph was made in 1979, scientists had no proof that comets ever collided with the sun. The bright round object in this photograph isn't actually the sun. It's a piece of equipment used to block out the sun's blinding center so that its outer edge can be studied.

Space dust. Scientists believe this bit of dust (above) came from a passing comet. Here, the dust has been magnified 15,000 times. Comet dust captured by the earth's gravity constantly drifts in the air. You cannot see it with the unaided eye, and it does no harm. Some probably fell on you today.

Have you ever acted really silly? Most people have at some time or other. When they do, their friends may laugh and say that they're acting loony.

The word loony suggests a connection between the moon and the way people behave. Loony is a changed and shortened form of lunatic, which means an insane person. Lunatic comes from the Latin word *luna*, or moon.

Long ago, people thought spells of insanity came and went as the phases of the moon changed. The phases depend on how much of the lighted side of the moon can be seen from the earth. When the moon is new, we cannot see it. When it is full, we see a ball.

Today, doctors know that the moon doesn't cause insanity. However, some scientists think there may be a link between the moon and human behavior. According to research conducted by a psychiatrist in Florida, the number of violent crimes goes up at the time of a full moon.

Scientists know that the strong pull of the moon's gravity affects many living things. Our moon is one of the largest satellites in the solar system. Its gravity tugs strongly at the earth, producing ocean tides.

The gravity of the sun affects the tides, too. However, the sun is farther away from the earth, so its pull is weaker.

It takes the moon about $29\frac{1}{2}$ days to go through all of its phases from one new moon to the next. As the moon's phases change, so do

A crescent moon hangs above a deserted beach near Acapulco, in Mexico. The picture was made a few days after the new moon—a period of high tides. At this time, the tides are gradually becoming lower.

CLIFF HOLLENBECK

the levels of the tides. At the time of the new and full moons, the sun, moon, and earth form a straight line in space. There's a big difference between high and low tides. The high tides are highest, and the low tides are lowest.

At the time of the quarter moons, the sun, moon, and earth form an L shape in space. The sun and the moon pull the oceans in different directions at the same time. The result: Tides that change less.

The moon and the tides affect the life cycles of many sea creatures. Some marine animals feed only at high tide.

Small fish called grunion lay eggs on a schedule determined by the tides. During six months of the year, thousands of grunion swim ashore for about four nights after a new or a full moon. Females quickly dig holes at the water's edge and lay eggs in them. Males fertilize the eggs. Then both males and females wriggle back into the sea.

Because the grunion lay eggs right after the highest tides, the eggs have a better chance of surviving. No high tides will disturb them while they are developing. If the eggs were laid at low tide, higher tides would uncover them and wash them away.

The grunion eggs stay safely buried in the sand until the next set of high tides arrives. That happens in about ten days, when the young are ready to hatch. The wave action triggers the hatching process. Then the waves sweep thousands of new grunion out to sea.

People don't respond to the moon and tides as obviously as grunion and other sea creatures do. But the moon probably has some effect on us, even if we aren't aware of it. That's one of the many reasons why scientists are taking a good look at the mysterious moon.

Fish dancers. Three grunion wriggle in soupy sand (right). Soon after the highest tides, grunion come ashore at night to lay eggs. Here, a female partly buries herself in sand. In less than half a minute, she lays thousands of eggs. Two males curl around her, fertilizing them. Then the fish return to the sea.

Fish watchers. John Bertsch, of the Cabrillo Marine Museum, in San Pedro, California, shows Timmy Durrell, 6, Sita Furnari, 12, and Stacey Durrell, 10, grunion laying their eggs on Cabrillo Beach.

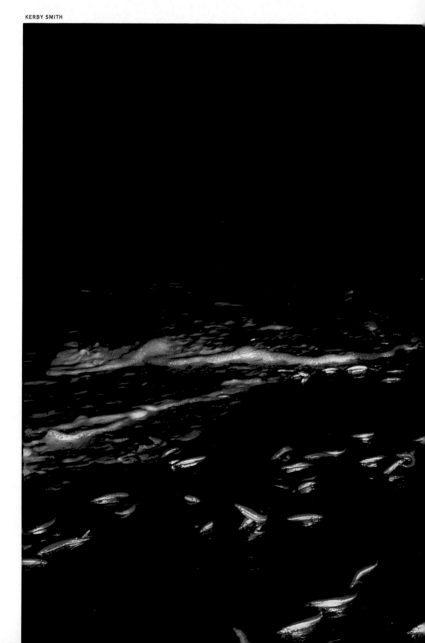

Grains of sand surround a cluster of grunion eggs (above). Each egg is smaller than the head of a pin. These eggs were uncovered for the picture, then covered up again so they would hatch.

CHAPTER 5

FACT OR FICTION?

People have always been good at "seeing things." A quick glimpse of an animal disappearing into the woods leads to stories of amazing creatures. Unusual lights in the night sky become floating UFOs. Sailors tell tales of sea monsters large enough to swallow ships. For centuries, many people firmly believed in unicorns such as the one on the right. The horn was thought to be a powerful medicine. Traders did a thriving business in unicorn horn. What they actually sold was a hornlike tooth from a narwhal, a small arctic whale. The word unicorn means "one horn." The narwhal, then, could be regarded as a unicorn. So could the Indian rhinoceros. Today, we know that the unicorn of legend doesn't exist. We know that fire-breathing dragons and ship-swallowing sea serpents do not exist. We also know that some animals people once thought were fictional—like giraffes and gorillas—are in fact real and alive. This chapter tells how scientists separate fact and fiction.

The profile of the Arabian oryx (above), an antelope that once lived in much of the Middle East, could have inspired tales of unicorns.
THE IMAGE BANK/AL SATTERWHITE

Centuries ago in Europe, artists "captured" this unicorn (right) in a tapestry. People believed the horn possessed magic powers.
METROPOLITAN MUSEUM OF ART/GIFT OF JOHN D. ROCKEFELLER, JR. THE CLOISTER COLLECTION, 1937.

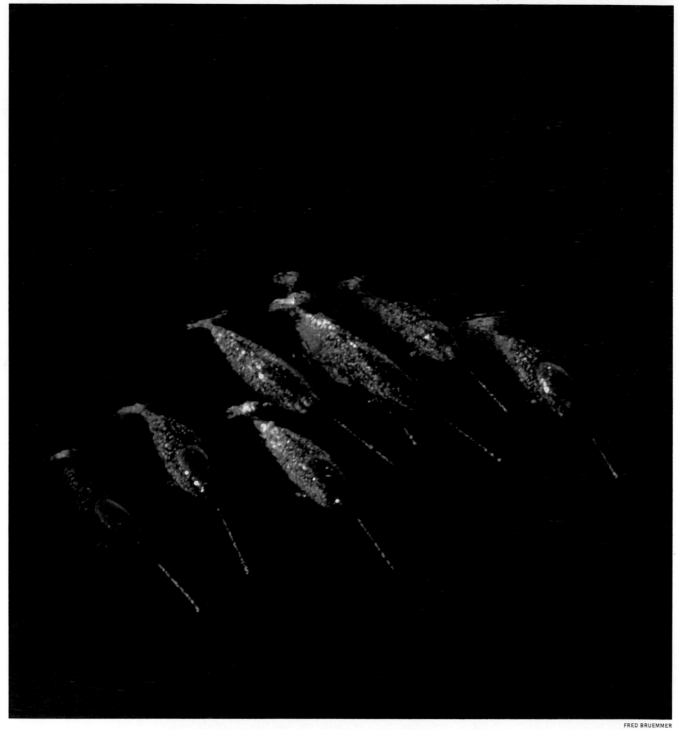

Narwhals swim in the Arctic Ocean. The "horn" of the male narwhal is really a tooth that reaches 5 feet (1.5 m) or more in length. When an English sea captain found a dead narwhal in 1577, he thought it was a marine species of unicorn.

MERMAIDS AND DRAGONS

Have you ever walked on a beach at night? It's not hard to imagine that you hear human voices whispering in the waves, or hear human arms splashing in the water.

Imagine what it must have been like to be a sailor when large parts of the world were unexplored. Your ship sails for weeks and weeks, often out of sight of land. Every now and then you might see a shadowy form near the shore or in the water near you. Could it be just a large fish—or might it be a creature with arms, half human and half fish?

Many seafaring people have told stories about mermaids. According to these stories, mermaids attracted attention by combing their long green and gold hair, or by singing strange, haunting songs. Far from home, sailors had to guard against certain mermaids that might lure them to watery graves.

What sea animals might have started people thinking about mermaids? Some sailors may have thought that the manatee, a large-bodied marine mammal with armlike flippers, resembled a woman. Christopher Columbus, in his ship's log, made a note that manatees were similar to creatures identified by sailors

J. MESSERSCHMIDT/BRUCE COLEMAN INC.

Relaxed on a rock, Hans Christian Andersen's "Little Mermaid" looks across the harbor in Copenhagen, Denmark. Many Danish stories tell of half-fish, half-human creatures reported by sailors.

FRED BRUEMMER

Could a marine mammal such as this northern sea lion sunning itself on a rock have made people think of mermaids? From a distance, it wouldn't be hard to confuse this sleek animal with a human form.

elsewhere as mermaids. Certain seals, also, might have looked human from a distance as they sunned themselves on rocks.

According to legends, dragons came from the sea to live in caves and on mountaintops everywhere. How did the idea of dragons start? A clue is that the word dragon comes from a Greek word meaning a large serpent. All dragons were snakelike. As time went on, parts of crocodiles, eagles, and other animals were added to the basic shape. Some dragons breathed fire; others could fly. In European legends, a hero always appeared to kill the evil dragon and make the people feel safe.

In Chinese legends, however, dragons usually were kindly. The Chinese as a rule did not fight their dragons. To them, the dragon represented wisdom and wealth.

JEN AND DES BARTLETT/BRUCE COLEMAN INC.

Real-life dragon, the Komodo lizard (above) lives on Komodo and nearby islands in Indonesia. It grows nine feet (3 m) or more in length, and has a forked tongue. It may have inspired the tales of Asian dragons. It resembles the dragon decorating a Chinese robe (right). The five claws indicate that the robe, woven three centuries ago, belonged to an emperor.

LEE BOLTIN

THE ATLANTIS STORY

Atlantis. To the ancient Greek writer Plato it was a beautiful island, the most beautiful on earth. The people were peaceful. The fields were rich with crops. The laws were fair.

But the people of Atlantis became greedy and dishonest. They angered the sea god who had given them the land and their laws. In his anger, the god caused the island to shake for one day and one night. Then it disappeared into the sea forever.

Was there ever such a place? Or did Plato invent the island of Atlantis to make a point in a discussion?

For many years, historians, archaeologists, geologists, and others have tried to find evidence of a place in the world that fits Plato's description. To him, Atlantis was a large island beyond the Pillars of Hercules, an ancient name for the Strait of Gibraltar.

Plato said that Atlantis, in a day and a night, was "overwhelmed by earthquakes" and "swallowed up by the sea." So some scientists searched for an island that had been shaken by a volcanic explosion in the distant past.

A Greek scientist decided that Thera, a Greek island in the Aegean Sea, must have been Atlantis. Recent studies suggest that Thera once had a large, flat central plain like Atlantis. Part of Thera had sunk into the sea after a volcanic eruption many times more powerful than that of Mount St. Helens, in the United States. And Thera had been part of an advanced pre-Greek civilization.

This painting shows Plato in the center with his hand raised high. The ancient Greek thinker described a beautiful island, Atlantis, that sank beneath the sea. Did he invent the story, or was there a real Atlantis?

VATICANO-STANZE DI RAFFAELLO

O. LOUIS MAZZATENTA, N.G.S. STAFF

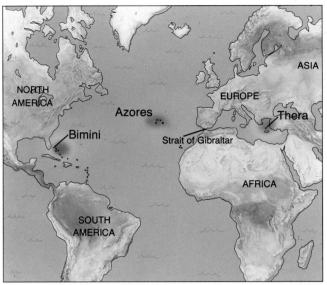

SALLY J. BENSUSEN

Plato described the splendid island of Atlantis about 2,400 years ago. People have searched for signs of it in many places. Three places show on the map above. The Azores and Bimini are located in the Atlantic. Volcanic eruptions created the Azores. Stone blocks in shallow water near Bimini look like a man-made road. The island of Thera lies in the Aegean Sea, a part of the Mediterranean. A huge volcanic eruption long ago plunged part of Thera into the sea.

N.G.S. PHOTOGRAPHER BATES LITTLEHALES

Calm lakes fill a volcanic crater on an island in the Azores (above). These islands lie in a location that suggests Atlantis, but little else about them fits the details of Plato's description.

A diver investigates blocks underwater near Bimini in the Bahamas (right). Scientists say these blocks are natural, rather than man-made, and were formed when beach sand hardened into stone. To others, the rows of blocks suggest a possible roadway in Atlantis.

The notion grew that Thera must have been the place Plato wrote about—even though the island is not on the Atlantic side of the Strait of Gibraltar. Another problem: Art found in ruins on Thera is not old enough to have been there when Plato says Atlantis existed—9,000 years before his own lifetime.

Plato wrote to teach people about his ideas. He was not a historian and did not always use facts to make his points. Perhaps Plato had a special reason that we don't know about for telling the Atlantis story exactly the way he did. Perhaps he made up the story, or perhaps he wrote down an old tale that had been passed along by word of mouth.

Thera today is also called Santorini. Many of the island's inhabitants live in this town. Steep cliffs fall to the sea, which flooded the island when part of it collapsed after a volcanic blast many centuries ago.

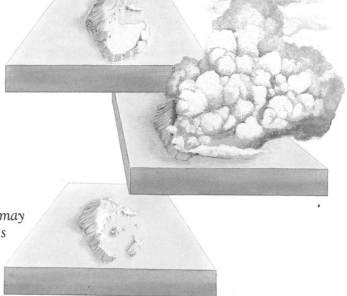

A volcanic blast sounded over the Mediterranean when Thera erupted. Top panel (right) shows how the island may have looked before the blast. Bottom panel shows today's look—with the sea covering the former flat central area.

88

Archaeologists have unearthed a ruin under 33 feet (10 m) of volcanic ash (left). Pots like these give clues to how people lived long ago on Thera. The search continues for any connection between Thera and Atlantis.

Long-haired boys box in a wall painting discovered on Thera (above). Archaeologists found the painting under layers of volcanic ash left behind by an eruption that some scientists think occurred in 1390 B.C. The painting helps prove that Thera was part of the thriving Minoan civilization that once ruled the Mediterranean.

89

MONSTER MEETING

Have you ever sat around a campfire and told monster stories? When you describe the scary creatures, you probably talk about how huge they are, how hairy, how frightening the red eyes and sharp fangs.

But have you ever actually seen one?

All around the world, people tell hair-raising stories about huge monsters that live in remote places. In the high Himalayas of Asia, some people still fear the Yeti, or Abominable Snowman. Sea monsters are said to swim in the oceans and in North American and European lakes and bays. Many North Americans have reported seeing a large, hairy, manlike creature called Sasquatch or Bigfoot.

So far, scientists have found no convincing proof that these creatures exist. All the tales have not been disproved to everybody's satisfaction, either.

Recently, an international group of serious researchers—people working in various branches of the natural sciences—banded together to form a society. Their group, the International Society of Cryptozoology, is dedicated to searching for scientific evidence of the many mysterious animals that people

Some of the mysterious creatures that people claim to have seen on earth gather in one imaginary spot. A Yeti carries a big stick on the far left. Sea monsters swim in the deep lake's waters. Overhead, a prehistoric pterodactyl flies again, as recently reported by tribespeople in Africa. In the right-hand corner sits Bigfoot. Serious searchers still look for signs to prove or disprove the existence of these creatures.

ROBERT E. HYNES

91

around the world claim to have seen. Crypto-zoology means hidden animal life.

For hundreds of years, people have reported seeing a strange water animal in Loch Ness, a deep lake in Scotland. They call it the Loch Ness monster—Nessie, for short.

Scientists think it *might* be possible for a group of large animals to live in Loch Ness and to be seen only rarely because the lake is so deep. A photograph made in 1934 shows what could be a serpentlike head rising from the surface. Recent studies, using underwater cameras and listening devices, have detected moving shadows that are not identifiable.

Many well-known organizations have supported efforts to find definite evidence of the Loch Ness monster. Until someone finds a live Nessie, or the actual bones or body of a dead one, the mystery cannot be solved.

People in the United States have reported their own versions of the Loch Ness monster. These include Champ, photographed in Lake Champlain, on the New York-Vermont border, and Chessie, reported in the Chesapeake Bay, in Maryland.

Brief movie footage of a large, hairy creature fleeing through a clearing in a northern California forest has been studied over and

"Here, Champ!" A Vermont vacationer took this picture of Lake Champlain's monster in 1977. Could it be a strangely shaped log? In the past 10 years, about 80 people have reported spotting Champ.

There it goes! In this picture (right), taken by a man who explored the California wilderness in search of Bigfoot, a hairy giant hurries away. Experts still debate whether this scene is faked or real.

93

over. Some experts say the scene shows a man in costume and was made as a joke. Others say the film shows a living descendant of a kind of giant ape that once lived in China. The creature is usually called Sasquatch in Canada and Bigfoot in the United States. Sasquatch is a name that comes from a word used by certain British Columbia Indians.

For a creature whose existence is questionable, Bigfoot seems to leave a lot of footprints. The prints have convinced at least some scientists that the animal exists. Others argue that marks looking like footprints might be faked or could have some other explanation.

Real evidence, such as a live creature or the bones of a dead one, is needed before the stories about these creatures can be proved or disproved. Animals unknown to science may still exist in remote areas around the world.

Pygmies in African jungles believe in the existence of an animal so monstrous that if they even talk about it, they will surely die.

But some brave Pygmies, when an exploring team showed them a picture of a *Brontosaurus*, called it by their own name for their local monster. Scientists know the Brontosaurus, a plant-eating dinosaur, lived millions of years ago. They have found its fossil remains. No scientist has found similar proof of an Abominable Snowman, or of Bigfoot, Nessie, Chessie, or Champ. If these monsters exist, they're very shy.

GORDON WILTSIE

| *A Sherpa painting shows a Yeti threatening a Himalayan village (above). Many people in Asia's high mountains are sure the Yeti exists. Scientists remain unconvinced.*

| *Mountain people in Asia believe Yetis leave prints like these (right). Scientists say a fox or other small animal made the prints. The snow around prints often melts, making them larger. The yard-long ice ax shows the size to which the sun has melted these prints.*

94

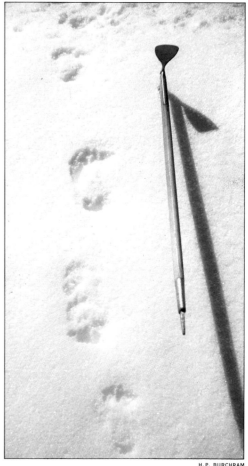

H. P. BURCHRAM

Travelers returning from central African jungles repeat stories of an amazing animal. Descriptions by tribespeople make the animal sound as if it could be a Brontosaurus. No such animal, nor any trace of a modern one, has ever been found, however.

ROBERT E. HYNES

SALLY J. BENSUSEN

Part of the Atlantic Ocean bounded by Bermuda, south Florida, and Puerto Rico has seen the disappearances of ships and airplanes. Called the Bermuda Triangle (above), the imaginary area has no borders. It exists mostly in the minds of those who like to have "supernatural" mysteries to think about.

Ship, ahoy. The Mary Celeste, *its crew gone (left), drifts near the Azores, a group of islands in the eastern part of the Atlantic Ocean. When sailors boarded the* Mary Celeste, *they found it deserted. No one knows for sure what happened. Stories range from a giant octopus that swept everyone overboard to a plot to kill the captain and capture the ship and cargo.*

ROBERT E. HYNES

Vast oceans cover much of the earth. Sailors may spend days at sea without sighting another ship. Long ago, sailors depended on stars to guide them. Today, radio equipment, compasses, and radar help guide sailors to port. And, almost always, ships reach port safely.

But in November 1872, the *Mary Celeste* sailed out of New York bound for Italy. Four weeks later, a British ship spotted the *Mary Celeste* off the coast of the Azores, in the eastern Atlantic Ocean. Something was wrong.

The *Mary Celeste* was drifting aimlessly, wallowing from side to side. No one could be seen on deck. When boarded, the *Mary Celeste* was found to be completely deserted. The cargo was all in place and there were no signs of violence. The lifeboat was missing.

What happened to the captain and crew of the *Mary Celeste?* No one seems to know. They just disappeared. They might have panicked, fearing the ship was about to blow up. Trying to flee in the lifeboat, they might have drowned when it turned over in rough seas. For years, the mystery has intrigued people, some of whom have suggested outlandish explanations for the disappearance.

The *Mary Celeste* mystery is often added to the mysteries of the so-called Bermuda Triangle, even though the ship was sighted far east of the map on this page. Larry Kusche, a leading expert, says the Bermuda Triangle is a "manufactured mystery" resulting from careless research or a desire to be sensational.

Ships and planes have been lost in the area called the Bermuda Triangle, but Mr. Kusche says that the disappearances can be explained by human error or bad weather—just as in any other similar-size area of the oceans.

97

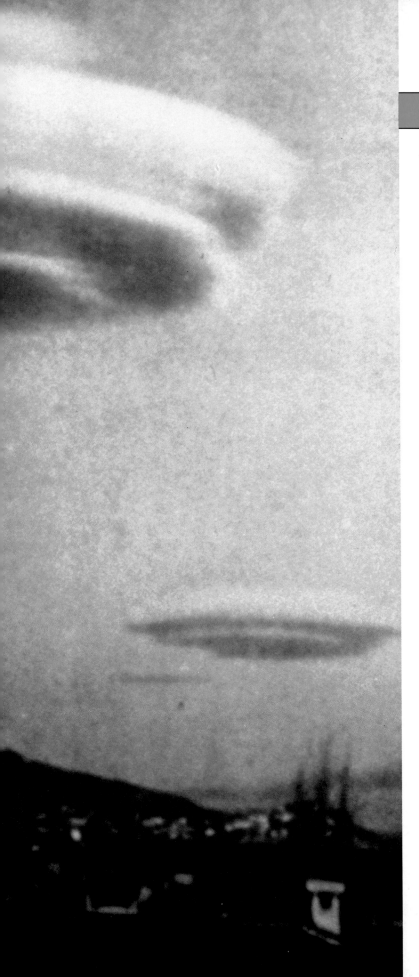

UFOs? OR CLOUDS?

Some experts believe that the people on earth are not the only intelligent form of life in the universe. With the likelihood of other solar systems in other galaxies, they argue, there must be other civilizations somewhere. Perhaps they are trying to communicate with us. We are trying to communicate with them. The United States space program has launched the space probes *Pioneer 10* and *Pioneer 11* with messages for any intelligent beings they might encounter in space.

Many serious scientists devote their careers to searching for radio signals from outer space, waiting to receive some that seem to come from an intelligent source. So far, they have heard only the natural radio signals of the stars and planets themselves.

Some people think that beings from space

DEPARTMENT OF PLANT PATHOLOGY, UNIVERSITY OF ARIZONA

Burn marks of a UFO landing? No, say scientists who study plants. This ring (above) is the mark of a fairy ring fungus, a kind of fungus that grows in a circle.

Saucer-shaped clouds over San Bernardino, California, look like a fleet of spacecraft (left). They're a special kind of cloud that forms when air is forced over hills or mountains. Clouds like this often stand still, as UFOs in movies sometimes do.

PHOTRI

99

have already appeared on or near the earth. Almost daily, someone reports seeing a UFO, an Unidentified Flying Object. Most of these "flying saucers" can be explained naturally. But some remain in question.

Scientists who study UFOs do not assume that the objects come from other parts of the universe. Many of them turn out to be such objects as weather balloons and satellites.

Clouds can also be confused with UFOs. Swamp gas may look like a spaceship's running lights. Camera flashes can cause light to show up on photographs, making people think they have taken a picture of a spaceship.

Science has explained many reported UFOs. But enough doubt remains to cause scientists to keep investigating—and learning more about—these amazing mysteries.

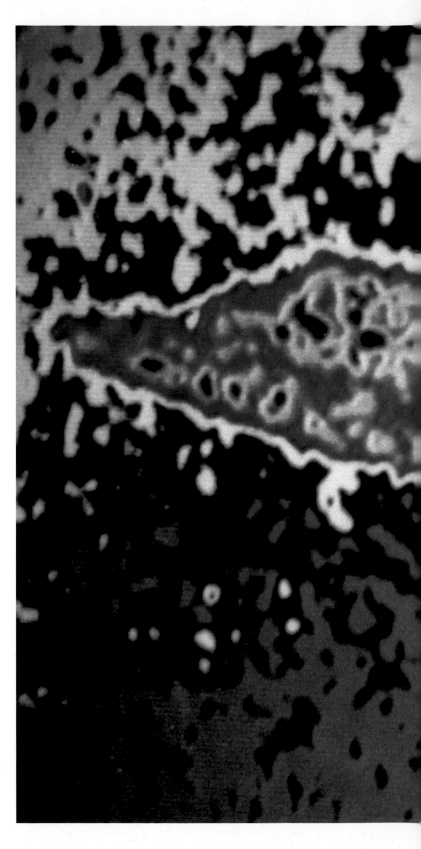

Up there in the circle—is it a pie tin, a Frisbee, or could it be a UFO? This picture (above) was taken on a farm in Oregon. Experts used a computer to process it. The computer image (right) shows nothing, such as a string, that could be supporting the solid object in the circle. The object itself remains unidentified.

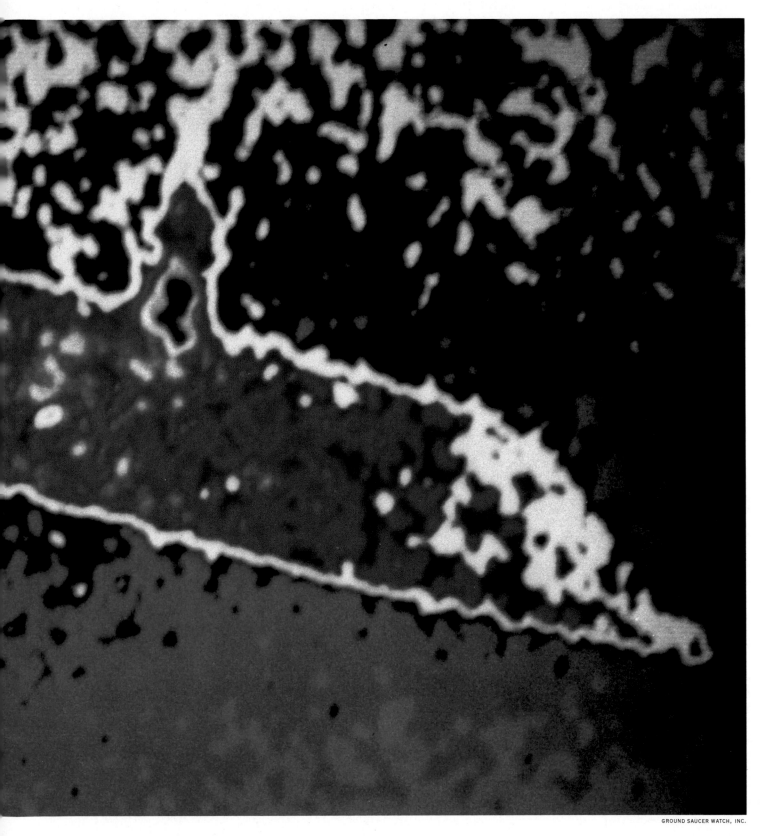

101

INDEX

Bold type indicates illustrations;
regular type refers to text.

ADDITIONAL READING

Readers may want to check the National Geographic Index and the WORLD Index in a school or a public library for related articles and to refer to the following books:

Children's Books

Anderson, Norman D., and Walter R. Brown, COMETS, METEORS, AND ASTEROIDS, Putnam's Sons, 1981. Anderson, Norman D., and Walter R. Brown, HALLEY'S COMET, Dodd, Mead & Company, Inc., 1981. Aylesworth, Thomas G., SCIENCE LOOKS AT MYSTERIOUS MONSTERS, Julian Messner, 1982. Beals, Carleton, THE INCREDIBLE INCAS: YESTERDAY AND TODAY, Abelard-Schuman Ltd., 1973. Blythe, Richard, DRAGONS AND OTHER FABULOUS BEASTS, Grosset & Dunlap, Inc., 1980. Branley, Franklyn M., BLACK HOLES, WHITE DWARFS & SUPER STARS, Harper & Row Publishers, Inc., 1976. Branley, Franklyn M., DINOSAURS, ASTEROIDS & SUPERSTARS, Harper & Row Publishers, Inc., 1982. Branley, Franklyn M., HALLEY: COMET NINETEEN EIGHTY-SIX, Lodestar Books, 1983. Branley, Franklyn M., THE MYSTERY OF STONEHENGE, Thomas Y. Crowell, 1969. Cohen, Daniel, THE WORLD OF UFOS, J. B. Lippincott Company, 1978. Colby, C. B., UNDERSEA FRONTIERS, AN INTRODUCTION TO OCEANOGRAPHY, Coward, McCann & Geoghegan, Inc., 1977. Fagg, Christopher, and Adrian Sington, HOW THEY BUILT LONG AGO, Franklin Watts, Inc., 1981. Gemming, Elizabeth, LOST CITY IN THE CLOUDS: THE DISCOVERY OF MACHU PICCHU, Coward, McCann & Geoghegan, Inc., 1980. Jaber, William, EXPLORING THE SUN, Julian Messner, 1980. Lampton, Christopher, BLACK HOLES AND OTHER SECRETS OF THE UNIVERSE, Franklin Watts, Inc., 1980. Lauber, Patricia, MYSTERY MONSTERS OF LOCH NESS, Garrard Publishing Company, 1978. Lyttle, Richard B., PEOPLE OF THE DAWN: EARLY MAN IN THE AMERICAS, Atheneum Publishers, 1980. Maynard, Christopher, THE YOUNG SCIENTIST BOOK OF STARS AND PLANETS, EMC Corporation, 1978. McMullen, David, MYSTERY IN PERU: THE LINES OF NAZCA, Raintree Publishers, Inc., 1977. Meyer, Miriam Weiss, THE BLIND GUARDS OF EASTER ISLAND, Raintree Publishers, Inc., 1977. Reiff, Stephanie Ann, SECRETS OF TUT'S TOMB AND THE PYRAMIDS, Contemporary Perspectives, Inc., 1977. Simon, Seymour, THE LONG JOURNEY FROM SPACE, Crown Publishers, Inc., 1982. Simon, Seymour, STRANGE MYSTERIES FROM AROUND THE WORLD, Four Winds Press, 1980. Smith, Howard E., Jr., LIVING FOSSILS, Dodd, Mead & Company, Inc., 1982. Thorne, Ian, BIGFOOT, Crestwood House, Inc., 1978. Wilkie, Katharine E., and Elizabeth R. Moseley, ATLANTIS, Julian Messner, 1979.

Books for Older Readers

Barry, James Dale, BALL LIGHTNING AND BEAD LIGHTNING: EXTREME FORMS OF ATMOSPHERIC ELECTRICITY, Plenum Press, 1980. Eather, Robert H., MAJESTIC LIGHTS: THE AURORA IN SCIENCE, HISTORY, AND THE ARTS, American Geophysical Union, 1980. Harris, John, WITHOUT A TRACE: A FRESH INVESTIGATION OF EIGHT LOST SHIPS AND THEIR FATES, Atheneum Publishers, 1981. Hathaway, Nancy, THE UNICORN, Viking Press, Inc., 1980. Hynek, J. Allen, THE UFO EXPERIENCE: A SCIENTIFIC INQUIRY, Contemporary Books, Inc., 1972. Kusche, Larry, THE DISAPPEARANCE OF FLIGHT NINETEEN, Harper & Row Publishers, Inc., 1980. Kusche, Lawrence David, THE BERMUDA TRIANGLE MYSTERY—SOLVED, Warner Books, Inc., 1975. Mackal, Roy P., SEARCHING FOR HIDDEN ANIMALS, Doubleday & Company, Inc., 1980. Mertz, Barbara G., RED LAND, BLACK LAND, Dodd, Mead & Company, Inc., 1978. Mertz, Barbara G., TEMPLES, TOMBS AND HIEROGLYPHS, Dodd, Mead & Company, Inc., 1978. Miller, Ron, and William K. Hartmann, THE GRAND TOUR: A TRAVELER'S GUIDE TO THE SOLAR SYSTEM, Workman Publishing, 1981. Moore, Patrick, SUNS, MYTHS AND MEN, W. W. Norton & Company, Inc., 1969. Oberg, James E., UFOS & OUTER SPACE MYSTERIES, Donning Company, 1982. Reader's Digest, THE WORLD'S LAST MYSTERIES, Reader's Digest Association, Inc., 1978. Singer, Stanley, THE NATURE OF BALL LIGHTNING, Plenum Press, 1971. Story, Ronald D., editor, THE ENCYCLOPEDIA OF UFOS, Doubleday & Company, Inc., 1980. Thorndike, Joseph J., Jr., editor, MYSTERIES OF THE PAST, American Heritage, 1977. Vitaliano, Dorothy B., LEGENDS OF THE EARTH, Indiana University Press, 1973. Wylie, Francis E., TIDES AND THE PULL OF THE MOON, The Stephen Greene Press, 1979.

National Geographic Books

EXPLORING OUR LIVING PLANET, 1983. EXPLORING THE DEEP FRONTIER: THE ADVENTURE OF MAN IN THE SEA, 1980. LOST EMPIRES, LIVING TRIBES, 1982. MYSTERIES OF THE ANCIENT WORLD, 1979. ON THE BRINK OF TOMORROW: FRONTIERS OF SCIENCE, 1982. OUR UNIVERSE, 1980. THE AMAZING UNIVERSE, 1975. THE INCREDIBLE INCAS AND THEIR TIMELESS LAND, 1975. THE MYSTERIOUS MAYA, 1977. THE OCEAN REALM, 1978.

Books for World Explorers (a National Geographic children's series)

AMAZING ANIMALS OF THE SEA, 1981. HIDDEN WORLDS, 1981. OUR VIOLENT EARTH, 1982. SECRETS FROM THE PAST, 1979. THE MYSTERIOUS UNDERSEA WORLD, 1980.

EDUCATIONAL CONSULTANTS

Glenn O. Blough, LL.D., *University of Maryland*
Lynda Ehrlich, *Montgomery County (Maryland) Public Schools*
Patricia Leadbetter King, Phyllis G. Sidorsky, *National Cathedral School*
Nicholas J. Long, Ph.D., *Consulting Psychologist*

The Special Publications and School Services Division is also grateful to the individuals and institutions named or quoted within the text and to those cited here for their generous assistance:

Thomas J. Ahrens, *California Institute of Technology*; Robert D. Ballard, *Woods Hole Oceanographic Institution*; J. Dale Barry, *Hughes Aircraft Company*; Peter T. Bartis, *American Folklife Center, Library of Congress*; Kay Brown, *Oregon Department of Fish and Wildlife*; Rhoda J. Bryant, *Florida State Museum*; John B. Carlson, *Center for Archaeoastronomy, University of Maryland*; Michael J. Crotty, *Los Angeles Zoo*; Robert H. Eather, *Boston College*; Charles H. Faulkner, *University of Tennessee at Knoxville*; Louis A. Frank, *University of Iowa*; Kenneth L. Franklin, *American Museum—Hayden Planetarium*; Robert K. Golka, *Project Tesla, Wendover Air Force Base, Utah*; Theodore R. Gull, *Goddard Space Flight Center*; Jessica A. Harrison, *Smithsonian Institution*; Nancy Berman Hathaway, *author of* THE UNICORN; James Heppner, *Goddard Space Flight Center*; Mary M. Holtan, *Oregon Department of Commerce*; J. Allen Hynek, *Center for UFO Studies*; Holger W. Jannasch, *Woods Hole Oceanographic Institution*; James A. Knowles, *Smithsonian Institution*; Larry Kusche, *author of* THE BERMUDA TRIANGLE MYSTERY—SOLVED; Robert A. Langel, *Goddard Space Flight Center*; David Lockner, *U. S. Geological Survey*; Bruce S. Maccabee, *Fund for UFO Research*; Roy P. Mackal, *University of Chicago*; Floyd W. McCoy, *Lamont-Doherty Geological Observatory of Columbia University*; Loren McIntyre, *author of* THE INCREDIBLE INCAS AND THEIR TIMELESS LAND; Thomas J. McIntyre, *National Marine Fisheries Service/NOAA*; Barbara G. Mertz, *author of* TEMPLES, TOMBS, AND HIEROGLYPHS *and* RED LAND, BLACK LAND; Daniel J. Milton, *U. S. Geological Survey*; J. Murray Mitchell, *National Oceanic and Atmospheric Administration*; John Dugan O'Keefe, *California Institute of Technology*; Richard E. Orville, *State University of New York at Albany*; Brian Partridge, *University of Miami*; Derek deSolla Price, *Yale University*; Emmanuel N. Rosales, *Cabrillo Marine Museum*; Sloan E. Schwindt, *Edge of the Cedars State Historical Monument, Utah*; Henry W. Setzer, *Curator of Mammals, Emeritus, Smithsonian Institution*; Bradford A. Smith, *University of Arizona*; Anna Sofaer, *The Solstice Project, Inc.*; Michael E. Stanghellini, *University of Arizona*; Ronald D. Story, *author of* THE ENCYCLOPEDIA OF UFOS; George E. Stuart, *National Geographic Society*; Robert M. Thornley, *Oregon Department of Commerce*; John A. Tilley, *The Mariners' Museum, Newport News, Virginia*; Dorothy B. Vitaliano, *U. S. Geological Survey*; H. Martin Wobst, *University of Massachusetts*.

Composition for AMAZING MYSTERIES OF THE WORLD by National Geographic's Photographic Services, Carl M. Shrader, Director; Lawrence F. Ludwig, Assistant Director. Printed and bound by Holladay-Tyler Printing Corp., Rockville, Md. Color separations by the Lanman-Progressive Co., Washington, D. C.; Lincoln Graphics, Inc., Cherry Hill, N.J.; NEC, Inc., Nashville, Tenn. Poster and FAR-OUT FUN! printed by McCollum Press, Inc., Rockville, Md.; *Classroom Activities* produced by Mazer Corp., Dayton, Ohio.

Library of Congress CIP Data
O'Neill, Catherine, 1950-
  Amazing mysteries of the world.
  (Books for world explorers)
  Bibliography: p.
  Includes index.
  Summary: Discusses such mystifying phenomena as the auroras, black holes, and Bigfoot.
  1. Curiosities and wonders—Juvenile literature.
[1. Curiosities and wonders] I. Title. II. Series.
AG243.053 1983   032'.02   83-13444
ISBN 0-87044-497-2 (regular binding)
ISBN 0-87044-502-2 (library binding)

AMAZING
MYSTERIES
OF THE WORLD

by Catherine O'Neill

PUBLISHED BY
THE NATIONAL GEOGRAPHIC SOCIETY
WASHINGTON, D. C.

Gilbert M. Grosvenor, *President*
Melvin M. Payne, *Chairman of the Board*
Owen R. Anderson, *Executive Vice President*
Robert L. Breeden, *Vice President,
Publications and Educational Media*

PREPARED BY THE SPECIAL PUBLICATIONS
AND SCHOOL SERVICES DIVISION

Donald J. Crump, *Director*
Philip B. Silcott, *Associate Director*
William L. Allen, William R. Gray, *Assistant Directors*

STAFF FOR BOOKS FOR WORLD EXPLORERS
Ralph Gray, *Editor*
Pat Robbins, *Managing Editor*
Ursula Perrin Vosseler, *Art Director*

STAFF FOR AMAZING MYSTERIES OF THE WORLD
Ralph Gray, *Managing Editor*
Alison Wilbur Eskildsen, *Picture Editor*
Lynette R. Ruschak, *Designer*
Carolinda Hill, Suzanne Nave Patrick, *Researchers*
Pat Robbins, *Contributing Editor*
Jane R. Halpin, *Editorial Assistant*
Gail N. Hawkins, *Picture Research Assistant*
Artemis S. Lampathakis, *Illustrations Assistant*
Janet A. Dustin, *Art Secretary*
Elizabeth M. Fisher, J. Michael Redmond,
 Alissa Sheinbach, *Interns*

STAFF FOR FAR-OUT FUN! Patricia N. Holland, *Project Editor*; Pat Robbins, *Text Editor*; Lynette R. Ruschak, *Designer*; Gloria Marconi, *Artist*

ENGRAVING, PRINTING, AND PRODUCT MANUFACTURE
Robert W. Messer, *Manager*; George V. White, *Production Manager*; Richard A. McClure, *Production Project Manager*; Mark R. Dunlevy, David V. Showers, Gregory Storer, *Assistant Production Managers*; Mary A. Bennett, *Production Assistant*; Julia F. Warner, *Production Staff Assistant*

STAFF ASSISTANTS: Nancy F. Berry, Pamela A. Black, Mary Frances Brennan, Nettie Burke, Mary Elizabeth Davis, Rosamund Garner, Victoria D. Garrett, Nancy J. Harvey, Joan Hurst, Rebecca Bittle Johns, Katherine R. Leitch, Virginia W. McCoy, Mary Evelyn McKinney, Cleo Petroff, Tammy Presley, Sheryl A. Prohovich, Carol A. Rocheleau, Kathleen T. Shea

MARKET RESEARCH: Mark W. Brown, Joseph S. Fowler, Carrla L. Holmes, Meg McElligott Kieffer, Nancy Serbin, Susan D. Snell, Barbara Steinwurtzel

INDEX: Dianne L. Hosmer